Stuart Yarnold

Windows 8.1
Tips, Tricks & Shortcuts

Covers Windows 8.1 Upate 1
and Windows RT 8.1 Update 1

W9-BYR-097

In easy steps is an imprint of In Easy Steps Limited
16 Hamilton Terrace · Holly Walk · Leamington Spa
Warwickshire · United Kingdom · CV32 4LY
www.ineasysteps.com

Notice of Liability
Every effort has been made to ensure that this book contains accurate
and current information. However, In Easy Steps Limited and the
author shall not be liable for any loss or damage suffered by readers
as a result of any information contained herein.

Trademarks
Microsoft® and Windows® are registered trademarks of Microsoft
Corporation. All other trademarks are acknowledged as belonging to
their respective companies.

In Easy Steps Limited supports The Forest Stewardship Council (FSC),
the leading international forest certification organisation. All our titles
that are printed on Greenpeace approved FSC certified paper carry the
FSC logo.

MIX
Paper from
responsible sources
FSC
www.fsc.org   FSC® C020837

Printed and bound in the United Kingdom

ISBN 978-1-84078-616-3

Contents

5 Things You Can Do Without 73

6 Customization 83

7 Paranoia 95

8 Security 107

9 Installation/Setting Up 123

10 Shortcuts 137

11 The Internet 147

12 Email 167

13 Multimedia 181

14 Miscellaneous 195

Index 211

1 Windows 8.1 Interface

Windows 8.1 features an interface called the Windows 8.1 Interface. While it has been designed primarily for use with touchscreen devices, it can also be used with standard screens. Here, we take a look at its main features.

Windows 8.1 is basically one operating system with two interfaces.

In order to serve its primary function of a mobile device interface, Windows 8.1 has been stripped of all unnecessary visual enhancements and menus.

What is the Windows 8.1 Interface?

The Windows 8.1 interface is a much-simplified (compared to the classic Windows interface) touchscreen interface of the type used in smartphones and tablets. Each installed program, or 'app' as they are known, is displayed on the Windows 8.1 Desktop, or Start screen, as a tile. While the ubiquitous icon does the same thing on the classic Windows Desktop, the main difference is that tiles can display live and constantly-updating content.

The apps themselves are also more streamlined than traditional programs and, accordingly, offer much less in the way of configuration options. The whole setup is designed to be clean, straightforward and quick, and thus much less demanding of system resources. Much of the eye-candy seen in Windows 7, such as Aero and transparent window borders has been removed.

This leads us to the rationale behind the interface. As two of the primary requirements for mobile devices are power efficiency and touchscreen control, its introduction clearly indicates that Microsoft considers mobile devices to be where the future lies.

Compatibility is another factor. Windows 8.1 will run on multiple platforms including smartphones, tablets, PCs and even the Xbox. This move toward cross-compatibility is one which is intended to establish Microsoft in the mobile market.

A key element in this is the OneDrive app. OneDrive enables users to store all their data and apps online and synchronize it across all their devices. As a result, they will be able to log into OneDrive on any Windows 8.1 device and access their data, apps and preference settings. Whatever or whoever's device they are using, it will be as though they are using their own.

There is a lot more to Windows 8.1 than just the interface, though. For example, it includes the older Windows 7 operating system as well. However, we'll start by taking a look at the various elements that comprise the Windows 8.1 interface.

Key Elements

The Lock Screen
The first thing you'll see when you start up is the Lock screen, which by default shows just the time and date.

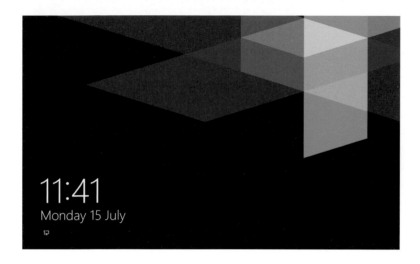

This screen is necessary because Windows 8.1 is a touch-supportive operating system and so requires a protective barrier to prevent accidental inputs. Microsoft has evolved this basic function by enabling users to customize the screen by changing its background and also by specifying various notifications to be displayed. These include the date and time as mentioned above.

Tap or click anywhere on the screen and the logon password box appears.

Start Screen
Having logged on, the user is then taken to the Windows 8.1 Desktop (also known as the Start screen). This is populated with a number of tiles, each of which represents an app. Some of these apps, such as Desktop and Video are static, whereas others are dynamic and are able to display updated content in real-time. Examples include the Email, Calendar and Weather apps.

To run an app, simply tap or click its tile. Tiles can be repositioned by dragging to a new location. When dragging a tile to the left or right, a gray bar will appear; if the tile is released on the far side of the bar, it will start a new group. This feature enables groups of tiles to be created.

Many Windows apps can be configured to display updated data in real-time on the Lock screen.

A lock screen is not necessary when Windows 8.1 is used with a non-touchscreen monitor. Many users will find it useful, though, purely as a means of displaying important information.

...cont'd

Tiles on the Windows 8.1 Start screen

Clicking the username at the top-right corner reveals options for changing the user picture, locking the PC, and logging out. The icons to the right of this reveal power options and a search box.

Menus

At first glance, the Start screen appears to be completely bereft of user options. There's no Start button, no Taskbar and no notification area. Right-click on the Start screen and all you see is a "Name groups" option (see below). However, most things are still available – you just need to know where to look. Microsoft, in its "keep it lean and mean" spirit, has stripped out many of the old options and changed the way much of what's left is accessed.

Right-click an empty part of the Start screen to reveal the "Name groups" option mentioned above. Click this and you'll see a "Name group" box appear at the top of each group of tiles. Click in a box and you'll be able to give the group a name. Click on the screen to return to the Start screen.

Right-click on the tiles themselves and you'll see menus offering options such as Resize, Pin to Taskbar, Unpin from Start, Uninstall, etc. These are contextual and so vary from app to app.

Hot tip

Menus in Windows 8.1 are more contextual than in previous versions of Windows, i.e. they now provide related options.

...cont'd

Right-click on the background of an open app and options bars open at the top and bottom offering related functions.

Charms Bar – The Charms bar is located down the right-hand side of the screen and, by default, is hidden from view. Hover the mouse over the top or bottom right-hand corners of the screen and the bar will appear as shown below.

On it you will find options to search your PC, share data, access other devices, and change settings on the PC. No matter where you are in the system, these universal options can always be accessed.

The Search function can be used to search for anything on your computer from applications to settings. Just open the Search app and start typing to search for any required item. The Share button allows you to view share options for the running application. Start takes you to the Start screen, Device allows you to access and change the settings of devices connected to your computer, while Settings provides access to a number of system options, plus access to further PC settings.

The Charms bar is context-sensitive, which means that it shows current application-related settings and options. It is also universal in that it can be accessed from anywhere, no matter which application is in use.

To access the Charms bar, hover the mouse over the top or bottom right-hand corners of the screen. Another way is to press Win + C.

The Windows key (or just "Win") is usually located at the bottom of the keyboard near to the space bar and often has an image of a flying window on it.

11

It's not actually necessary to open the Search app to do a search. Simply start typing while on the Start screen and the app will open automatically.

...cont'd

Application Switch List – The top left-hand corner also activates a menu. Hover the mouse over the corner while on the Start screen and the Switch list will appear as shown below:

This shows all apps currently running on the PC down the left-hand side of the screen. To switch to a different app, simply click on it in the list.

Power User Menu – When on the classic Windows Desktop, right-clicking on the Start button opens a menu of options likely to be of interest to advanced users. This is shown below:

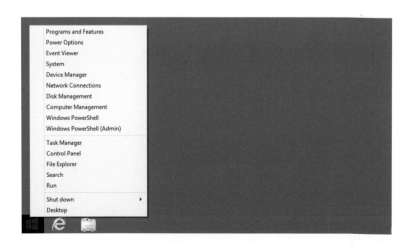

If you wish to access the Power User menu while on the Start screen, press Win + X. This also works on the classic Windows desktop.

Left-clicking on the Start button takes you to the Start screen.

Navigation

In its drive for Windows 8.1 to be all-encompassing, Microsoft has made it possible to manipulate the interface in three different ways: by touch, mouse and keyboard.

Touch

Touch gestures include swiping, sliding, tapping and pinching. The best way to get to grips with these is to experiment. The following, however, will get you off to a good start:

Swipe from the right – moving a finger from the right-hand side of the screen to the left opens the Charms bar.

Swipe from the left – moving a finger from the left-hand side of the screen to the right opens the Application Switch list, which shows all the open apps and enables the user to switch between them.

Swipe slowly from the left – by performing the above left-to-right action more slowly, it is possible to drag an app out of the Switch List and "snap it" to run side-by-side with the current app.

Swipe down from the top – moving a finger from the top of the screen to about halfway down will close the current app.

Swipe down – swiping down from the top of the screen brings up an option to view all the apps and programs installed on your PC, not just the Windows 8.1 apps. When performed in an open app, the same movement reveals related options. For example, in the Internet Explorer app, it opens a tab menu that shows a list of all open tabs, plus a new tab button.

Swipe down on a tile – this selects an app and at the same time opens the Options bar at the bottom of the screen.

Pinching and stretching – pinching enables the user to zoom out on the Start screen or an open app. Stretching zooms in.

Slide left/right – sliding a finger to the right of the screen scrolls across the Start screen. Sliding it left, scrolls back. The same movements in the Internet Explorer app open the next and previous pages.

Tapping – this action is used to select an option or to open an app.

The old Windows Task Switcher (Alt + Tab) can also be used to show open apps.

In many cases, the touch commands available are dependent on the application in use. For example, various rotational commands can be used to manipulate objects in drawing and layout applications such as Microsoft PowerPoint.

Hot tip

Spinning the mouse wheel while on the Lock screen will open the password box. When on the Start screen, it scrolls the screen.

...cont'd

Mouse

Using the mouse to get around in Windows 8.1 is no different to any other operating system. The trick is knowing where to position the mouse to reveal the menus and features provided by the interface. We have covered this in pages 9-12.

Keyboard

Those of you who use the Start screen without the benefit of a touchscreen are well advised to get acquainted with the various keyboard commands relevant to it. In many cases, just as with keyboard commands and shortcuts in general, they are often quicker than using the mouse.

There are actually a whole bunch of these commands and a full list is shown on pages 144-146. The following are some of the more useful ones:

The key that will be used most is the Windows key, also called WinKey – see page 146. Pressing this key instantly returns the user to the Start screen regardless of where they are. It can also be used in conjunction with other keys to perform other actions. For example, Win + X opens the Power User menu as mentioned on page 12, while Win + C opens the Charms bar.

The Home and End keys jump from one end of the Start screen to the other, while the arrow keys can be used to select a tile. The Enter key opens an app.

Tapping the space bar opens the options bar at the bottom of the screen. Win + Tab opens the Application Switch list that allows the user to switch to a different app. While the list is open, pressing the Delete key closes the apps in turn. Alt + Tab opens a horizontal version of the Application Switch list. Note that you must have at least two apps running for Win + Tab and Alt + Tab to work.

Press Ctrl + Tab to open a list of all apps and programs installed on the computer and cycle through the list with the arrow keys.

A rarely-used key known as the Context Menu key (usually located close to the space bar) brings up a menu of related options when pressed in an open app. This appears at the top of the app window.

Organization

Windows 8.1's tiles are quite bulky and take up a lot of screen real estate. Therefore users with a large number of apps will find themselves having to constantly scroll across the Start screen unless they get their apps organized.

There are two ways to do this: The first is to arrange the apps in order of frequency of use so that the most frequently-accessed are located on the visible part of the screen. This can be done by individually selecting tiles and dragging them to the left side of the screen. The second is to reduce the size of the tiles – do this by right-clicking on a tile and clicking Resize. Depending on the app, you'll have options for Small, Medium, Wide and Large.

Another obvious user requirement is to have apps organized into related groups. Again, this can be done by dragging and dropping tiles. However, this is a laborious way of moving groups of apps.

A much quicker way is to select an app group and drag and drop the entire group. The way to do this is by making use of Windows 8.1's Semantic Zoom feature. Touchscreen users can "spread out" and, if you're using a mouse, press the Ctrl button while rotating the mouse wheel. Both actions reduce the size of the tiles as shown below:

Hot tip

A new app group can be created by dragging an app to the right until a gray divider bar appears. Release the app at this point and the new group is created.

15

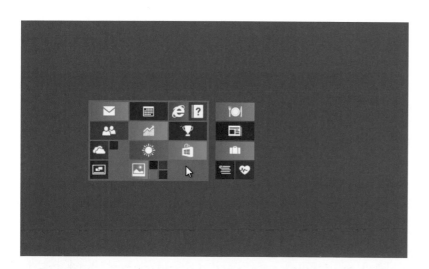

Hovering the mouse over an app group automatically selects the whole group, which can then be dragged to a new location and released.

Apps

In keeping with Microsoft's intention of making inroads into the mobile market, the apps created for Windows 8.1 are very similar to the apps found in tablets.

The first similarity regards the way the apps display content in real-time. For example, there is a weather app that shows a constantly-updated ten-day forecast and a news app that displays current stories and images.

The second is simplicity. As with the Windows 8.1 interface itself, Microsoft has designed the apps to be clean and straightforward with the minimum of extraneous clutter – the app's content is intended to dominate. A consequence of this is that the traditional navigational aids such as toolbars, menus, preview panes, etc, are in evidence to a much lesser degree.

To use Microsoft terminology, the apps are "immersive applications" – which basically means they run in full-screen mode. For users with a large, wide-screen monitor this is definitely a restriction. However, this is mitigated to a certain extent by a feature called Snap. This makes it possible to have up to four apps running side-by-side – we explain how to set this up on page 68.

Traditional Windows programs will still work in Windows 8.1. However, because they have not been optimized for it, they can only be used in classic Windows, which is where the user will be automatically switched to when they are run.

It's important to be aware that Windows 8.1 apps are different to their classic Windows equivalents. For example, two versions of Internet Explorer are provided in Windows 8.1 – an Internet Explorer app and the classic Internet Explorer. While the latter supports plugins and add-ons, the app version doesn't.

Sourcing and Installing Apps

In order to provide as secure a computing environment as possible, official Windows 8.1 apps are only available from the Windows Store.

This effectively "sandboxes" them and, as a result, users are much less likely to introduce viruses and malware to their computers via downloaded software.

Hot tip

Unless specifically closed by the user, Windows 8.1's apps are always open, even if the user has switched to a different one. However, unlike with previous Windows versions, this has a negligible effect on a PC's performance. This is due to the fact that system resources allocated to the app are automatically reduced to a level just enough to keep it running.

Hot tip

It is possible to install third-party apps on Windows 8.1 – see page 66.

To access the Windows Store, click the Store tile on the Start screen. You will then be asked to sign in with your Microsoft account.

17

The first thing you'll see is a carousel showing large images of five featured apps. To the right of this is a list of top categories followed by a section called Picks for you, which shows a number of apps of the type often used by the user. For example, if you play a lot of card games, this section will feature card game apps. Moving along, there are sections showing trending apps, new and rising apps and top paid and top free apps.

At the top of the screen is a search box. Using it activates three filters – All categories, All prices and Sort by relevance. The category list can also be accessed by right-clicking on the screen.

On each app's page, there are ratings and reviews to the right of the main image. Next to these are sections for Details, Related apps, and other apps from the manufacturer. At the left are Buy or Install buttons (this option is available if the app is free). Below is the price, description and the app's features.

Once you've chosen and paid for an app, just click the Install button. It will then be downloaded and installed automatically. Once this has been done, the app's tile will be placed at the end of the Start screen, from where it can be dragged to the desired position.

…cont'd

Closing Apps

Closing an app is very simple to do once you know how, but, as many users have discovered, the method of doing so is far from obvious.

Before we go any further with this, it must be pointed out that usually it is not actually necessary to close apps. This is because when a new app is opened, other running apps are switched to a state of suspension in which they use very little in the way of system resources.

However, there may be situations in which it is desirable or even necessary to close down an app. The following are three ways to do this:

- Simply press ALT + F4 – this kills the app instantly

- Move the mouse to the top of the screen and a title bar will appear. Click the X to close the app and the - to minimize it

- Type Task Manager and you'll see the Task Manager icon appear. Click this to open the utility and select the Processes tab where you'll see a list of all running apps and programs as shown below:

Don't forget

Most of the time, it is not necessary to shut down an app. Due to the way that Windows 8.1 minimizes the system resources required by apps that aren't being used, you can, in fact, have a whole bunch of apps running at the same time without any noticeable degradation of system performance.

Hot tip

A quick way of opening the Task Manager is to press Ctrl + Shift + Esc.

Task Manager						
File Options View						
Processes	Performance	App history	Startup	Users	Details	Services
			0%	32%	1%	0%
Name		Status	CPU	Memory	Disk	Network
Apps (4)						
▷ 🅔 Internet Explorer			0%	15.2 MB	0 MB/s	0 Mbps
Mess	Expand		0%	36.1 MB	0 MB/s	0 Mbps
▷ Sticky	End task		0%	2.2 MB	0 MB/s	0 Mbps
▷ Task	Resource values ▶		0%	7.2 MB	0 MB/s	0 Mbps
Backgrou	Create dump file					
COM	Go to details		0%	1.3 MB	0 MB/s	0 Mbps
COM	Open file location		0%	0.8 MB	0 MB/s	0 Mbps
Device Association Framework …	Search online Properties		0%	2.6 MB	0 MB/s	0 Mbps

Right-click the app you wish to close and select "End Task".

2 Performance

Windows operating systems require a powerful computer in order to function at their best. Those of you whose systems are struggling to run Windows 8.1 will be able to achieve a higher level of performance by implementing the measures described in this chapter. We also explain some more general performance-boosting steps that apply to all versions of Windows.

Overview

Operating systems, no matter how good they may be, are completely reliant on the hardware used to run them. If the hardware is not up to the job, while the operating system may function, it will not do so at its best.

If your PC can run Windows Vista or Windows 7, it will run Windows 8.1 just fine.

Even where the hardware is good enough, if it is configured or installed incorrectly, the operating system will be adversely affected. On a slightly different tack, it is often possible to squeeze a bit more performance from a hardware device by tweaking its settings.

In this chapter, we look at these issues and show how to get both your computer and operating system running at their maximum performance level.

Your hardware is the place to start and the good news is that Windows 8.1 does not require anything out of the ordinary in this respect. If your computer can run either Windows Vista or Windows 7, it will also run Windows 8.1 without the need for any upgrading.

However, if you do experience any problems, or would simply like to get your computer running as well as possible, there are quite a few adjustments that can be made to the default settings, which will make it run considerably faster. For users whose hardware provides a performance level that is on the borderline between poor and acceptable, these can negate the need for a hardware upgrade.

If your system struggles with Windows 8.1, there are steps you can take to reduce the demands made by it.

There are also some more general steps that users can take in order to keep their system running, not just at peak performance but also reliably. These are not specific to Windows 8.1; they apply to any operating system.

This chapter shows the tweaks that can be made to Windows 8.1 default settings to improve its performance, and also shows, generally, how to keep your PC running smoothly and reliably.

Please note that in this book, unless otherwise mentioned, we are concentrating on the Classic Windows interface as is used on traditional mouse controlled desktop PCs rather than the Windows 8.1 interface, which is really only suitable for handheld devices and touchscreen monitors.

Add More Memory

Without any doubt, the quickest and most effective method of improving the overall performance of a computer is to simply increase the amount of memory it has.

Windows 8.1 will not function well with any less than 1GB of memory. Optimum performance will require 2GB.

So how do you go about doing this? It is, in fact, a very simple procedure that takes no more than a few minutes but does require the system case to be opened. Once this has been done, you will see a large circuit board facing you at the right-hand side of the case. This is the motherboard and at the top-right, you will see the memory sockets containing the memory modules as shown below:

Open the retaining clips and insert the new module by pressing down on the top edge until the retaining clips close automatically

If one or more of the sockets are empty all you have to do is fit extra modules to complement the existing ones. If the sockets are all in use, you will have to remove some, or all, of the modules and replace them with modules of a larger capacity.

However, if the prospect of meddling inside the case doesn't appeal to you there is an easier, although less effective, option available. This is called ReadyBoost and is explained on the next page.

To find out how much memory your PC has, open the System Information utility by pressing the Windows key + R. In the Run box type MSINFO32. On the system summary page scroll down to Total Physical Memory.

You cannot install just any memory – it has to be compatible. Consult your PC's manual to see which type you need.

Memory modules must be handled very carefully. Before touching one, ground yourself by touching the metal case chassis. If you don't, the electrostatic charge in your body could well damage the module.

Quick Speed Boost

If Windows were to run out of memory, the PC would literally grind to a halt. To prevent this, it uses a paging file on the hard drive as a memory substitute. The problem with this is that hard drives are much slower than memory, so performance is reduced when the paging file is being used.

The solution is to prevent Windows having to use the paging file, and the way to do this is to install more memory. However, many users don't know how to install memory; plus, it is expensive.

ReadyBoost will not work with just any flash drive – it must be a good quality model.

ReadyBoost provides an easier and cheaper alternative. All you need is a USB flash drive with a capacity of between 256MB and 4GB. Plug the drive into a USB port and a message will pop up asking you to decide what to do with the drive. Click the message and then select "Speed up my system" as shown on the right.

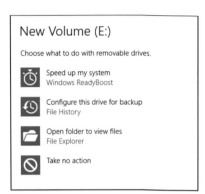

New Volume (E:)

Choose what to do with removable drives.

Speed up my system
Windows ReadyBoost

Configure this drive for backup
File History

Open folder to view files
File Explorer

Take no action

ReadyBoost enables you to increase your system's performance without having to buy and install more memory. It is also a much cheaper option, as flash drives are half the price of memory of equivalent capacity.

1 Select "Use this device"

2 Specify the space to reserve for ReadyBoost. Then click Apply

Windows will now use the USB drive as a cache for the most commonly-paged data. The paging file will still be on the hard drive but will be used much less.

Users with less than 1GB of physical memory will benefit the most from using ReadyBoost.

The minimum amount of flash memory you can use for ReadyBoost is 256MB. The maximum amount is 4GB. We suggest at least 1GB.

22

Reduce the Visual Effects

Windows comes with a number of visual effects, e.g. fading or sliding menus, drop shadows, pointer shadows, etc. These are all designed to improve the look and feel of the Windows interface.

They do, however, add nothing to its functionality. In fact, they can, and do, have a negative impact on the system. Remember: each of these effects consumes system resources.

Users interested in performance rather than appearance will benefit from disabling some, or even all, of these essentially unnecessary graphic enhancements:

1 Press Win + X to open the Power User menu. Click Control Panel, System, Advanced system settings

2 Click the Settings button under Performance

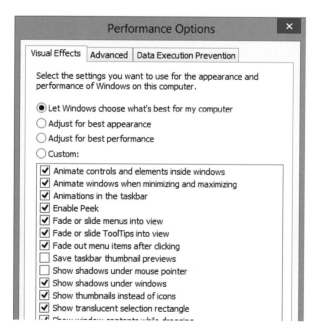

3 Select "Adjust for best performance"

By default, Windows chooses the first option "Let Windows choose what's best for my computer", which enables the majority of the effects. You can disable them all as shown above. Alternatively, you can disable them individually.

Hot tip

Windows visual effects are purely cosmetic and serve no practical purpose. Disabling them will have no effect on the PC's functionality.

Beware

Disabling all of the effects will have a significant impact on the appearance of the classic Windows interface.

Icon Thumbnails

By default, Windows displays all file icons as thumbnails (mini graphical representations). This is particularly useful when viewing image files, as it enables you to see the image without having to first open it in an imaging program as shown below:

However, there is a downside. Because graphic files take longer to open than any other type of file, having this feature enabled does adversely affect system performance. Users who want their system to run as fast as possible, and those who simply need a performance boost, will benefit by disabling this feature. Do it as described below:

1 Go to Control Panel, Folder Options. Then click the View tab

2 Check the "Always show icons, never thumbnails" check box

Faster Paging

When Windows runs out of physical memory, it uses a special file on the hard drive as a substitute, known as the paging file. Moving it to a different drive speeds up the paging operation, and thus system performance (see top margin note). To carry out this procedure you will, of course, need two hard drives:

1 Go to Control Panel, System. Click System Protection and then the Advanced tab

2 Click Settings (under Performance) and then the Advanced tab. Under Virtual Memory, click Change

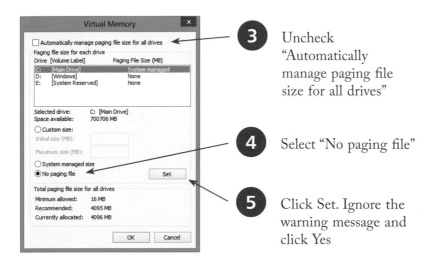

3 Uncheck "Automatically manage paging file size for all drives"

4 Select "No paging file"

5 Click Set. Ignore the warning message and click Yes

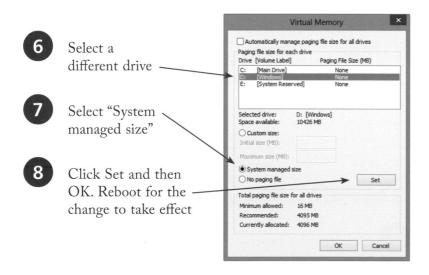

6 Select a different drive

7 Select "System managed size"

8 Click Set and then OK. Reboot for the change to take effect

Hot tip

A separate drive that doesn't have Windows and other applications installed on it will be more responsive as it is used much less than the main drive. So, placing the paging file on it will improve the speed of the paging operation.

25

Hot tip

There is no benefit to be gained by moving the paging file to a different partition on the same drive. It must be moved to a separate drive.

Disable Superfetch

The Superfetch feature in Windows helps to keep the computer consistently responsive to your programs by making better use of the computer's memory.

Windows Superfetch prioritizes the programs you're currently using over background tasks, and also adapts to the way you work by tracking the programs you use most often and preloading these into memory. As a result, they open much more quickly when accessed.

On PCs that have 2GB or more of memory, Superfetch works very well. However, if your PC has less than 2GB it can lead to excessive disk thrashing (see margin note) and sluggish system performance. The less memory you have, the worse the effect.

If you find yourself in this position, you have three options:

● Upgrade your memory so you have at least 2GB

● Enable ReadyBoost – see page 22

● Disable the Superfetch feature

The latter is done as follows:

1 Go to Control Panel, Administrative Tools. Click Services and scroll down to the Superfetch service

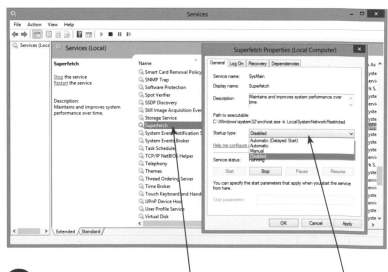

2 Double-click Superfetch and in the Startup type drop-down box, select Disabled

Hot tip

Disk thrashing occurs on PCs that are low on memory. Because of the lack of memory, the operating system has to frequently utilize the hard drive as a memory substitute. This leads to data being constantly transferred between the hard drive and the memory.

Beware

Disk thrashing can damage or cause premature failure of the hard drive due to excessive wear and tear on the read/write heads.

Cancel Unneeded Services

When a Windows PC is being used, in the background and unseen by the user, a number of applications known as Services will be running. While many of them are essential for certain functions of the operating system, there are some that are not.

As every running application makes a hit on system performance, this is something you will want to prevent. Fortunately, you can override Windows and make the decision yourself as to which services should be running. As a guide, the services specified in the list on the right can be disabled safely. The procedure for doing so is exactly the same as described on the previous page (Disable Superfetch).

However, should you consider disabling any services that are not listed on the right, we suggest that you first take a look at what the service does and also what other applications may be depending on it. Do this as follows:

1 Open the service's Properties dialog box where you will see a description of the service's function

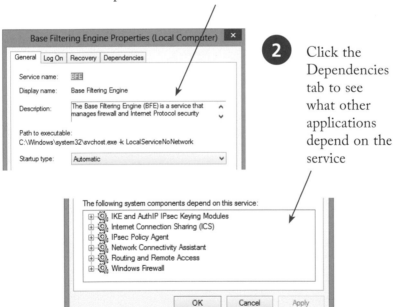

2 Click the Dependencies tab to see what other applications depend on the service

By checking this out, you will not inadvertently disable a service that is essential to the running of your PC.

Hot tip

Services that can be disabled are:

- IKE and AuthIP IPsec Keying Modules
- Remote Registry
- UPnP Device Host
- WebClient
- Windows Error Reporting Service
- Windows Image Acquisition (WIA)

If you don't use your PC for networking, the following can also be disabled:

- Computer Browser
- Distributed Link Tracking Client
- Netlogon
- Network Access Protection Agent
- Peer Name Resolution Protocol
- Peer Networking Identity Manager
- SSDP Discovery
- Server
- TCP/IP NetBIOS Helper
- Workstation

More Shutdown Options

There are several ways to access a Windows 8.1 PC's power off options: You can do it from Settings on the Charms bar, and by right-clicking the Start button and selecting Shut down. Shut down options are also available at the top-right of the Start screen. All these methods provide limited options, however.

Here is a another way that also restores the Log Off (Sign Off), Switch User, and Sleep options. Do it as follows:

1 On the Start screen, open Search and type "notepad". This opens the Windows Notepad application

2 In Notepad, type the following:

```
dim objShell
set objShell = CreateObject("shell.application")
objshell.ShutdownWindows
set objShell = nothing
```

3 From the file menu, click Save As and in the box enter a suitable name, e.g. Shut Down. Give it the .vbs file extension as shown below and save it to the desktop

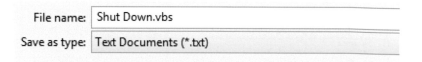

Assuming you use the example above, you will now see a Shut Down icon on the desktop. Click it and the traditional Windows Shut Down dialog box will be revealed as shown below:

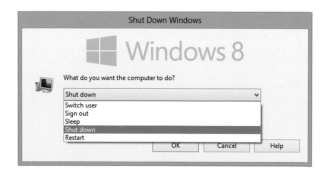

You can drag your new Shut Down icon to the taskbar where it can be quickly accessed.

Streamline the Registry

The registry is a central hierarchical database that holds all of the important Windows settings regarding software, hardware and system configuration. It also provides a common location for all applications to save their launching parameters and data.

Over time, as the user installs and deletes programs, creates shortcuts and changes system settings, etc., obsolete and invalid key information builds up in the registry. While this does not have a major impact on a PC's performance, it can be the cause of system and program errors that can lead to instability issues.

The solution is to scan the registry periodically with a suitable application that will locate all the invalid entries and delete them.

While Windows Registry Editor is adequate for editing purposes, it does not provide a cleaning option. However, there are many of these applications available for download from the Internet. A typical example is Registry Mechanic (shown below). These programs provide various options, such as full or selective scans, backups, the creation of System Restore points, etc.

Beware

Changes to the registry can be dangerous. So create a system restore point using the System Restore utility first – see page 208. If you have any problems as a result of the change, you will be able to undo it by restoring the system.

29

Occasional use of a registry cleaner will help to keep your system stable and thus, more reliable.

Optimize the Hard Drive

Assuming you're not already using one, a very good way of improving not only drive performance but that of the whole PC, is to replace the boot hard drive (the one Windows is installed on) with a solid state drive (SSD).

To do this will mean opening up the system case, which is something many users will not be comfortable with. However, if you are prepared to do it, or know someone who can do it for you, the benefits are considerable.

The main one is speed – the Seek time of an SSD (the time it takes to locate a file) is in the order of .01 ms compared to around 7 ms for a traditional mechanical hard drive. The result is a computer that is effectively turbo-charged – boot times, typically, are halved and programs open instantaneously.

SSDs are also far more reliable than mechanical drives as they contain no moving parts. This means that it is much safer to store data on an SSD. Other advantages include their small dimensions, low power requirements, and no need for maintenance (defragmentation).

The only real drawbacks of these devices is the cost – two to three times as much as a mechanical drive, and relatively low storage capacity. For these reasons, the use of SSDs is usually restricted to the boot drive, with a mechanical drive providing much larger and cheaper data storage capacity.

Installing an SSD is actually a very simple operation. All that is required is to a) secure the device in place, and b) connect the data and power cables to the drive. You'll then need to install a clean copy of the operating system on the drive, or copy it from the existing drive. Full installation and setting up instructions are usually supplied with the devices.

Keep it Lean and Mean

When approximately 70% of a hard drive's storage capacity has been used, its performance level will start to decrease. It will also be more likely to be affected by the issue of fragmentation.

So, when it begins to approach this mark, you should start thinking about freeing up some space. As it's a sure fact that many of the files on your drive will be redundant, you can usually do this without losing anything important:

1 Go to Control Panel, Administrative Tools. Click Disk Cleanup on the left-hand side

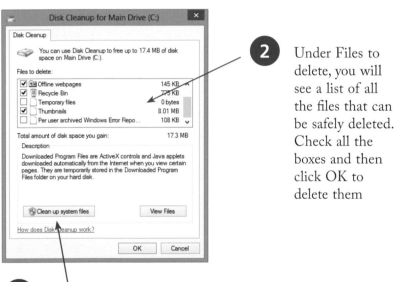

2 Under Files to delete, you will see a list of all the files that can be safely deleted. Check all the boxes and then click OK to delete them

3 Click Clean up system files. You'll see a list of system files that can be deleted. Delete these as described above

The next thing to delete is System Restore points. As these are actually system backups, they are very large files, often several GBs in size, and there may be several of them. Do it clicking the More Options tab in Disk Cleanup and then clicking Clean up under System Restore and Shadow Copies.

Finally, click Clean up under Programs and Features. You'll see a list of all the programs installed on the PC. Go through the list and uninstall any that you don't use. You'll now have even more xdisk space.

The more data you have on your drive, the worse the effects of fragmentation.

System Restore points are created whenever major changes are made to the system. These points can occupy a tremendous amount of disk space, so deleting them is worth doing. The action on the left deletes all but the most recent restore point.

...cont'd

Keep the File System Healthy

Over time, especially if the PC is well-used, file system and data faults can build up on the hard drive. Not only can these have an adverse effect on the PC's performance, they can also be the cause of general system instability, and thus potential loss of data.

To correct these types of faults, Windows provides a disk maintenance utility called Chkdsk. Access it as follows:

1 Press Win + X to open the Power User menu. Select File Explorer, which opens This PC

2 Right-click the drive you want to check and select Properties. In the window that opens, click the Tools tab

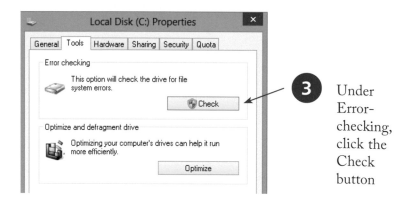

3 Under Error-checking, click the Check button

Windows 8.1's version of Chkdsk will usually alert the user when it needs to be run. However, regardless of whether or not you get an alert, we recommend you run it after every incorrect shutdown or system crash. These are the actions that will introduce file system errors to the hard drive. If you don't do this, one of these days your system may simply refuse to boot up.

4 Click Scan drive. If Chkdsk finds any errors on your hard drive it will attempt to repair them

Hard Drive Speed Boost

This tip shows how to boost hard drive speed, and thus system performance, by implementing a hard drive configuration technology known as RAID (Redundant Array of Independent Disks). This is a way of configuring a combination of hard drives to gain specific benefits; in this case, an increase in drive speed.

To set up a RAID configuration, you will need two hard drives and a RAID controller. With regard to the latter, most modern motherboards provide one; check your motherboard documentation to see if yours does – if so, you're all set. If it doesn't, you'll need to buy a RAID controller PCI card, which you install in a PCI slot on the motherboard.

When you have installed the second hard drive, boot the PC and then press the key specified in the motherboard documentation to open the RAID utility.

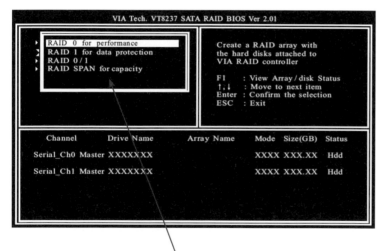

Typically, you will be given four options: RAID 0, RAID 1, RAID 0/1 and RAID Span – see margin notes.

To make the task easier, most RAID setup utilities offer an auto-setup option. All you have to do is specify the configuration required, which in this case is RAID 0. The utility will then set up the configuration automatically; the process taking only a few seconds. Reboot and you're done.

Go to This PC and you will see just one drive. Its capacity, however, will be the combined capacities of the two drives.

A RAID 0 configuration splits the data across the drives. As each drive handles half the work load, data transfer rates are much improved. However, if either of the drives fail, all of the PC's data will be lost.

A RAID 1 configuration copies data to each drive. The advantage here is security – if one drive fails, the data is recoverable from the other one. The drawback is that the capacity of one of the drives is lost.

A RAID 0/1 configuration is basically a combination of RAID 0 and RAID 1. It offers the benefits of both but requires at least four hard drives. RAID Span is merely a way of combining two drives into one – there's no real benefit from it.

Update Device Drivers

First, what exactly is a driver? Well, let's assume that you are about to print a document and have opened your printer software to change a few settings. What you are looking at is actually a driver, in this case your printer's driver.

A driver has three purposes: some, like the printer driver mentioned above, act as an interface between the device and the user, allowing changes to be made to the way the device operates.

Second, all drivers act as an interface between their device and the operating system. They tell the operating system what the device needs in terms of system resources for correct operation.

Third, drivers provide a way for hardware manufacturers to update their devices to take account of advances in technology, both hardware and software.

Unfortunately, drivers can cause problems, particularly when they are used with a new operating system (this invariably introduces technologies that the driver's devices were not designed for). In most cases they will install without problems and the devices will appear to be functioning. However, behind the scenes the drivers may well be the cause of incompatibility issues that can lead to both instability and loss of system performance.

In an effort to prevent this, Windows displays a warning message when it detects that a potentially problematic driver is being installed. However, it is a fact that most users ignore these messages and install the driver regardless.

If you've done this yourself, you should be aware that you may well have compromised your system.

So to be quite sure that the PC is running at its best, you must uninstall all non-certified Windows drivers and replace them with ones that are. To do this:

1 Go to Search on the Charms bar and type 'verifier'

2 Click the verifier link under the search box to open the utility

Hot tip

Upgrading your device drivers is not just important with regard to the operating system – in many cases, the devices themselves will perform better as a result.

Hot tip

Drivers that are certified for use with Windows have been tested by Windows Hardware Quality Labs (WHQL). They are commonly referred to as "signed drivers" as they have been digitally tagged as such.

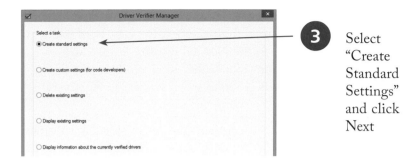

3 Select "Create Standard Settings" and click Next

4 In the next dialog box, select "Automatically select unsigned drivers" and click Next

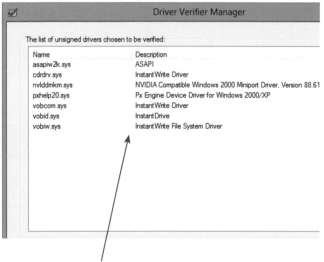

5 In the final dialog box, you will see a list of all the unsigned drivers on the PC

While they are probably OK, these drivers are all potential causes of system problems. Therefore, if you want to be absolutely certain that your computer is as stable, and performing as well as possible, you will have to either replace them all with Windows-certified versions, or uninstall them.

To this end, visit the websites of the devices' manufacturers and look for updated drivers certified for use with Windows 8.1. Download and install them. If a manufacturer doesn't provide a Windows 8.1 driver, ideally you should replace the device with one from a manufacturer that does.

Many users assume that system crashes and lockups are due to faults in the operating system. The reality is that the majority of them are caused by uncertified hardware drivers or low-quality memory.

If you can't find a Windows 8.1 driver, one designed for use with Windows 7 will almost certainly be OK.

Prioritize CPU Resources

"Priority" is the measure that Windows uses to determine the amount of CPU time that each application receives. By default, most applications are set to the Normal priority level, so by changing a specific program to a higher level you can effectively boost its performance. This is useful when you are using several applications simultaneously (multi-tasking).

Do the following:

1 Run the program to be prioritized

2 Open the Task Manager (Ctrl + Shift + Esc)

Beware

The highest priority setting is Realtime. This will give an application the same priority as critical system services. We recommend that you do not use this, as doing so can render your system unstable.

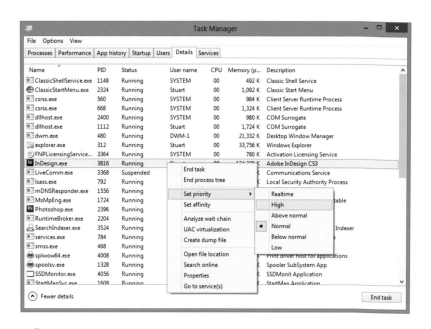

3 Open the Details tab and locate your application. Right-click on it and go to Set Priority. You'll see options ranging from Low to Realtime. Select the one you want and close the Task Manager

Hot tip

You can also set lower priority levels for your applications. As an example, if you have an open program that is accessed infrequently, giving it a lower priority will increase the CPU resources available for more frequently-used applications.

Note that changes to priority level are not permanent; they are effective only while the program is running. If you close it and then open it again, it will have reverted to the default setting.

Third-Party Software

Having tweaked Windows to give improved performance, you should now look at your PC's applications. These can also be the cause of performance issues.

Program Overload

The first thing to examine is the number of programs you have installed. The more there are, the slower your PC is going to be, even if they are not being used. If this puzzles you, be aware that many applications (or parts of them) run unseen in the background. So the more software you install, inevitably the more of these background applications there will be. Not only do they slow system performance, they also affect shutdown and startup speeds. Do this as described on page 31. Alternatively, go to Programs and Features in the Control Panel.

Malware

Malware is a term that encompasses invasive software, such as adware, spyware and browser hijackers. Quite apart from compromising your PC's security and intruding on your privacy, they can also slow your Internet activities considerably and, in the case of hijackers, can have a real impact on the PC's performance.

Windows 8.1's answer to this problem is the Windows Defender utility, which is enabled by default. In theory, this application should keep your system clean of all viruses and malware. In practice, however, it is unlikely to do so. Just as email spammers are constantly devising new ways to circumvent spam filters and other safeguards, the authors of viruses/malware are doing the same with anti-virus programs.

You have two ways to approach this problem: prevention or cure. To prevent malware getting on to your PC, avoid:

- Downloading anything from the Internet unless you are quite sure about the source

- Browsing the Internet with any of Internet Explorer's security features turned off

- Installing software from unverifiable sources

If you must do any of the above, or already have, scan your system with anti-virus and anti-malware programs.

Hot tip

No anti-malware program is perfect, so to ensure your system is as clean as possible, we suggest you use at least two. We recommend Spybot Search & Destroy (available from www. safer-networking. org) and Malwarebytes (available from www. malwarebytes.org). Both provide free versions.

Refresh the PC

There comes a time in the life of any well-used computer when it will benefit hugely from a good clear out. Over time, files are created and deleted, programs are installed and uninstalled, the inevitable crashes occur, and users do things they shouldn't. A PC can become clogged up with redundant and useless data, long-forgotten files, programs, and broken shortcuts. Furthermore, essential system or program files may have gone missing or been corrupted. At best this will be the cause of irritating little faults and problems and, at worst, a serious decrease in system performance or loss of functionality.

There is absolutely nothing that can be done about this, no matter how carefully you maintain the PC. Traditionally, the only effective solution to this problem has been a clean install, i.e. backing up all the data on the PC, reformatting the hard drive (which wipes the drive clean), installing a new copy of Windows, and then reinstalling the backed up data and programs.

It is a procedure that returns the PC to an "as new" condition but does require a level of technical expertise that most users simply don't have. However, Windows 8.1 includes two utilities that simplify this issue considerably: Refresh Your PC and Reset Your PC. Here, we are going to look at the Refresh Your PC utility. We look at the latter on page 205.

Access the utility by going to the Charms bar, Settings. Then select "Change PC Settings" and click "Update & Recovery". Click "Recovery" and on the right you'll see a "Refresh your PC without affecting your files" option. Click "Get Started" underneath it and you will then see the following screen:

Hot tip

Virtually all problems that occur with Windows can be repaired. However, it is almost always easier to simply revert the system to a state prior to the fault manifesting itself. Windows 8.1 provides two tools with which to do this.

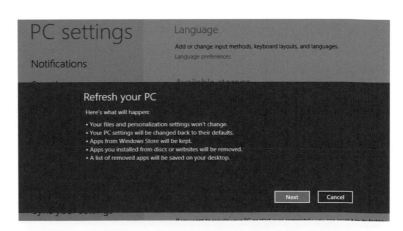

This tells you what will happen if you run the utility:

- **Your files and personalization settings won't change** – this means that your data will not be deleted, and that any changes you have made to the default personalization settings will be retained. The former is the big plus here as it means you do not have to make a backup of your data and then reinstall it afterwards.

- **The PC's settings will be changed back to their defaults** – this means that Windows 8.1 will be deleted and replaced by a new copy. Any configuration changes made to Windows settings will be lost.

- **Apps from the Windows Store will be kept** – apps installed from the Windows Store will not be deleted.

- **Apps you installed from discs or websites will be removed** – all third-party software will be deleted.

Effectively then, the Refresh Your PC utility will install a new copy of Windows 8.1 while retaining the user's apps, data and personalization settings. Everything else will be deleted. The big drawback is that users will probably have to reinstall/reconfigure most of their software, and reconfigure various Windows settings. That said, it will still be much quicker than doing a clean install as described on pages 125-126.

However, by utilizing a little-known command line utility known as recimage.exe, it is possible to create a customized image of the system that is automatically associated with the Refresh Your PC utility. When the latter is run, it restores the system from the image.

By creating this image *after* all desired third-party software has been installed and the computer set up to the user's requirements, it is possible to use the Restore Your PC utility to completely return a computer to the state it was in when the image was created – reinstalling software and reconfiguring Windows settings will not be necessary. To do this:

1. Create a folder (it doesn't matter where) and give it a suitable name, e.g. "backup". Make a note of the drive letter (e.g. C:) of the drive the folder is located on

Hot tip

A big advantage of the Refresh Your PC utility is that it is quick. It will reinstall Windows in a fraction of the time taken by the original installation.

Hot tip

By itself, the Refresh Your PC utility is just an enhanced way of reinstalling Windows. By using it in conjunction with a custom image it becomes a much more powerful tool.

…cont'd

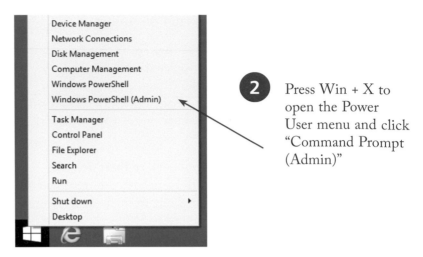

2 Press Win + X to open the Power User menu and click "Command Prompt (Admin)"

Hot tip

In Step 3, the letter C is the drive letter of the drive your backup folder is located on. If you are using a drive other than the c drive, change this accordingly, e.g. d:\backup.

3 At the prompt, enter the following:
recimg -createimage c:\backup. Then press Enter

```
Windows PowerShell
Copyright (C) 2013 Microsoft Corporation. All rights reserved.

PS C:\Windows\system32> recimg -createimage c:\backup
Source OS location:  C:
Recovery image path: c:\backup\CustomRefresh.wim
Creating recovery image. Press [ESC] to cancel.
Initializing
100%
Creating snapshot
100%
Writing image (this may take a while)
100%
Registering image
100%

Recovery image creation and registration completed successfully.
PS C:\Windows\system32> _
```
Administrator: Windows PowerShell

The utility will first create a snapshot or image of the system, which takes a few seconds. It will then write the image to the specified drive and folder (the C: drive and backup in the example above). This may take some time to complete, depending on the amount of data being imaged. The final step is associating (registering) the image with the Refresh Your PC utility.

This is all done automatically and once done, should the user decide to subsequently run the Refresh Your PC utility at some point, the computer will be restored to the exact state it was in when the customized image was created.

3 Startup & Shutdown

Don't you just hate it when your PC insists on taking its own sweet time to start up and shut down? The procedures in this chapter will teach it some manners and ensure that its laggardly ways are a thing of the past.

Disable Unused Hardware

Every time a computer is switched on, its hardware has to be detected and initialized by the BIOS. Thus, the more devices there are, the longer the PC takes to boot-up.

While most of the PC's hardware is essential for it to run, in virtually all systems there are some devices that are not used. By disabling these, you can increase the PC's boot speed:

1 Go to Control Panel, Device Manager. Here, you will see a list of all the hardware installed on your system

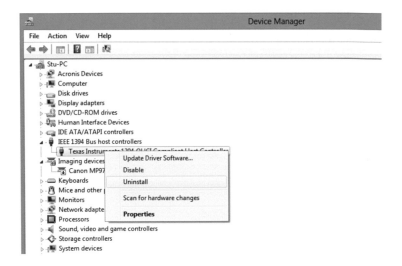

2 Go through the list (don't forget to expand the various categories) and disable any devices that you do not use. Do this by right-clicking the device and clicking Disable

Examples of devices that are typically unused include:

● **Network adapters** – most motherboards provide an integrated network adapter

● **Bluetooth controllers** – if you don't use Bluetooth (and very few people do), you don't need to have it enabled

● **Multimedia devices** – integrated video and sound. Many users have dedicated sound and video cards so don't need these

Streamline the Fonts Folder

Windows comes with a large number of fonts, all of which are installed in the Fonts folder. As each of these fonts is loaded when the PC starts up, the more there are the longer startup takes to complete. Therefore, you can increase your boot speed by deleting all but the ones used by the system, and the ones *you* are likely to use:

1 Open the Windows folder on the C: drive and locate the Fonts folder. Right-click it, select Copy and save it in a backup location

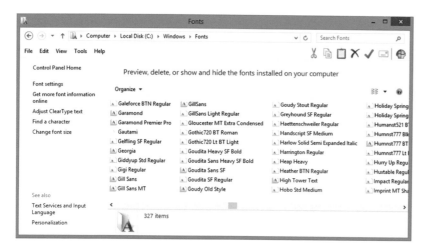

2 Now open the original folder and simply work through the fonts, deleting any that are surplus to requirements; this should be the vast majority of them

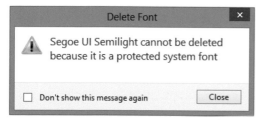

Note that some of the fonts are system fonts and are used by the operating system. If you try to delete any of these, you will see the "cannot delete..." message shown above. Should you subsequently find a need for any of the deleted fonts, just copy them back to the Fonts folder from your backup folder.

Hot tip

A font manager can be very useful for users who access the fonts on their systems regularly. These can be downloaded from the Internet.

Beware

Be wary of downloading free fonts from the Internet. These are often corrupt and may cause your system to lock-up completely.

45

Clear Out the Startup Folder

The next thing to look at is your startup programs. These are applications that open automatically when Windows starts and are located in the Startup folder.

Beware

The more programs you
have in your Startup
folder, the longer the PC
will take to boot.

Items can be placed here by the user if he or she wants them to open with Windows, so they are ready for immediate use. Also, some programs will place a link here automatically when they are installed.

As each of these programs must be loaded before Windows is ready for use, the more there are in the Startup folder, the longer it will take.

Check it out as follows:

1 Right-click the taskbar and click Task Manager. The Task Manager utility will open

2 Click the Startup tab. You'll see a list of applications that start with Windows as shown below:

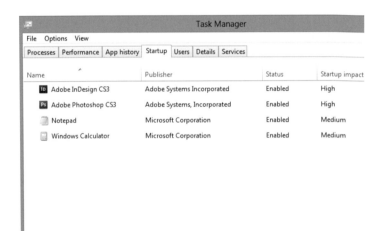

3 For maximum speed gain, simply disable everything

However, if there is something you'd rather keep, check the Startup impact column to see the impact it has on the PC's startup speed. If it says low there is really no need to disable it as its effect will be minimal.

Screensavers and Wallpaper

In days gone by, computer monitors were prone to having an impression burnt into the screen by prolonged exposure to a static image. To guard against this unfortunate tendency, screensavers were invented. Quite apart from serving a useful purpose, they could also be fun.

These days, however, that's all they are – fun. They are now completely superfluous in the modern computer system, as monitors are no longer susceptible to damage caused by static images.

Because a screensaver is actually a program, having one enabled means that Windows has one more application to load before it is ready to use. So reduce your PC's startup time by disabling any screensaver that is currently active. Do it by right-clicking the desktop and clicking Personalize. Then click Screen Saver, and in the next dialog box select None from the drop-down box.

Be wary of using any of the 3D screensavers available on the Internet. Not only can they take a long time to load, they can also contain bugs, and cause system instability.

With regard to wallpaper, these are large image files that have no function other than to make your Desktop look cool. As with screensavers, they slow down the startup procedure as they also have to be loaded by Windows.

Your best option here is to use a solid color as the background. Right-click the desktop, select Personalize and then Desktop Background. From the drop-down box, select Solid colors.

Shutdown issues can be difficult problems to identify. Device drivers are the most likely cause and this is what you should investigate first.

The Event log will also highlight issues that are causing your PC to boot more slowly than it should.

Shutdown Issues

When a Windows PC takes an unusually long time to shut down, the cause is almost always one of the following:

- A service, or running process, that is slow to close
- The unloading of user-profile files
- A non-responding application
- A corrupted or incompatible device driver

The first three in the list above have, to a certain degree, been addressed in recent versions of Windows, and therefore do not cause as many problems as they did with earlier versions. That said, on occasion, they are still the cause of shutdown issues.

Device drivers are beyond Windows' control as the decision of whether to install a particular driver is down to the user. Windows will warn the user if it thinks a driver being installed is potentially problematic but it cannot stop the installation. This is the biggest cause of shutdown problems with Windows (see pages 34-35 for how to eliminate driver issues).

When in this situation, go to the Control Panel and open Administrative Tools, Component Services. On the left go to Event Viewer (Local), Applications and Services Logs, Microsoft, Windows, Diagnostics-Performance. Click Operational.

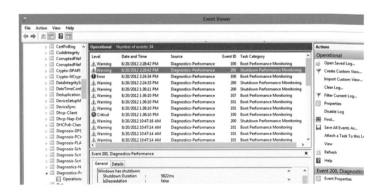

Look under the Task Category for issues relating to Shutdown Performance Monitoring. Clicking an entry will reveal details of the application that is causing a delay in the shutdown process. Click the Event Log Online Help link, and you will be taken to a Microsoft website where you may find more detailed information.

Kill Services Quickly

When a PC's shutdown button is pressed, Windows closes all open applications, including any services that may be running. The length of time Windows allocates for the latter is set by the WaitToKillServiceTimeout registry key; the default setting of which is 5000 ms (5 seconds).

If all running services stop within 5 seconds, the PC shuts down. However, if they don't, the user is presented with a dialog box, which offers two options: wait for the service to stop of its own accord or force it to close.

By lowering the default value, you can force tardy services to close more quickly and thus prevent them from slowing down the shutdown procedure.

Press Win + R, type "regedit" in the Run box and press Enter. Windows Registry Editor will open. Navigate to the following key:

HKEY_Local_Machine/System/CurrentControlSet/Control

Click the Control folder on the left and then on the right you will see the WaitToKillServiceTimeout key.

Beware

Resist the temptation to set too low a value as this may lead to loss of data. Services do need some time to close. The object here is simply to speed up the process somewhat.

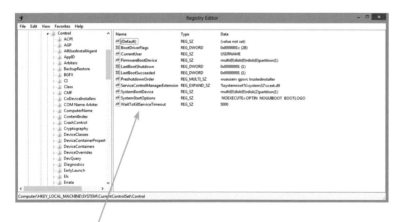

Double-click the key and in the Edit String dialog box that opens, enter a lower value

Put the PC to Sleep

Windows provides an option for closing down your machine known as "Sleep". This is accessible by pressing CTRL + ALT + DEL and clicking the power icon at the bottom-right. You can also access it from the power options at the top-right of the Start screen.

The Sleep power mode is basically a combination of the old Standby power mode and Hibernate mode.

In Hibernate mode, an image of the system is created on the hard drive and then the PC is powered off. The problem is that, in practice, it is not much quicker than just switching off and then back on as normal.

In the old Standby mode (not available in Windows 8.1), an image of the system was created in memory and power was maintained only to essential devices such as the CPU. The problem here was that an application could override Standby and keep the PC running. Also, if power to the PC was lost for some reason, e.g. a power blackout, all unsaved data was lost.

Windows Sleep mode saves all data in use to both the memory *and* the hard drive before cutting power to all but a few key components. The procedure takes just a few seconds. When a key is pressed, the mouse moved or the screen tapped, the system is restored from the image stored in the memory. If the machine has been powered off, the system is restored from the image stored on the hard drive on restart. Thus, there is no danger of data loss.

Furthermore, and this is the major advantage of Sleep, it is quick, taking approximately three seconds to bring the PC back to life.

Sleep mode eliminates the need to switch a computer off between sessions at all. Simply put the machine to sleep at the end of the day, and then have it up-and-running within three seconds the following morning with a single keystroke or mouse click.

Hot tip

On laptops, Sleep mode only saves an image to the memory – not to the hard drive as well. It then monitors the battery and if it runs low, transfers the image stored in the memory to the hard drive.

(4) Productivity

Computers can be used for both entertainment and work. In this chapter we focus on the latter, looking at ways to increase the efficiency with which you use your computer. These will help you to save time, and also be more productive.

Find it Fast

An important part of working efficiently and productively is being able to locate things quickly when needed. The workman who can lay his hand on the right tool when needed will get the job done faster than the one who has to go looking for it.

Working on a PC is much the same, so to make life easier for users in this respect, Windows 8.1 provides a Search utility. This is tightly integrated in the operating system and thus is instantly accessible from virtually any location. You will find it in any Explorer folder and on the Charms bar.

One of its best features is that it is contextual, i.e. its search is based on the user's current activity, whether it's searching for utilities in the Control Panel, or for files and applications on the hard drive.

Folder Searches

If you already know in which folder the file is located, use the search box at the top-right of the folder. By default, the search will be restricted to the contents of the folder. You will also see an option for searching all subfolders of the current folder. Next to this is an option for searching the entire computer – use this when you have no idea where to look.

Also available are filters, which help to speed up the search – these appear on the menu bar when you click in the search box and enable you to search by various criteria, such as date, size, kind, etc. See page 55 for more on filters.

Windows 8.1 Search

The search function is also available from the Windows 8.1 interface. Just begin typing your query and it will open. The results are displayed below the search box as shown in the screenshot on the next page.

Don't forget

By default, a folder search will only find content that is located in the folder in which the search is conducted.

Hot tip

When using the Windows 8.1 interface, there is no need to open the Search utility from the Charms bar. Simply start typing and Search will open automatically.

If you have any information regarding a file you're looking for, using it in conjunction with search filters will enable the file to be located more quickly.

Search Aids

Windows 8.1 provides two very useful tools that enable the user to increase the efficiency with which the Search utility is used.

File Indexer

The first is the Indexing utility. When the operating system is run for the first time, it creates an index of all the files in the most commonly-used locations (note, not the entire computer). As a result, subsequent searches are much faster as Windows searches the index rather than the computer.

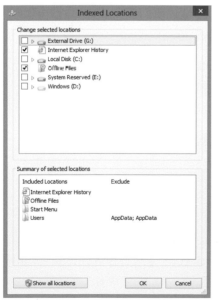

However, users who are in the habit of scattering files all over the place, or adding storage devices to the PC, e.g. a second hard drive, can configure the utility to index any location they wish, or even the entire system.

To do this, go to Control Panel, Indexing Options. Click Modify and then select the locations to be indexed.

If you decide to index the entire computer, be aware that the procedure can take several hours. During this time, system performance may be adversely affected. This only needs to be done once though, so it's not a major deal.

You can add multiple tags to a picture. To separate tags, type a semicolon (;) between each tag.

Don't
forget

The Tag feature does not work with all file types. Microsoft file types, e.g. .doc or .docx (Word), and image files work but files from many third-party applications do not.

...cont'd

Tags

Tags provide a method of invisibly marking selected files. This makes the procedure of subsequently finding, and organizing them, much quicker and more efficient. Tagging is particularly useful on computers that have lots of images stored on them.

Use this feature as follows:

1 Open the folder containing the file to be tagged, click the View tab and then click Details Pane on the menu bar

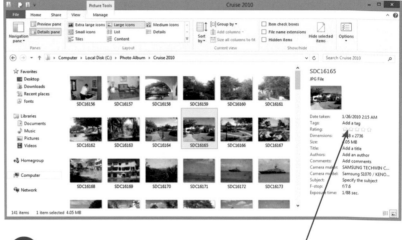

2 Select the file, click Add a tag and enter an appropriate word or phrase. Then click Save

Another way to tag a file is to right-click it, select Properties and open the Details tab. Then select Tags and press any key – this will open a text entry box alongside as shown below:

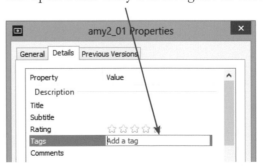

Type your tag into the box. You can also add or change other properties in the same way, e.g. Title, Comments, etc. These all give you extra options when doing a search.

Advanced Searching

Searching in Windows 8.1 can be as simple as typing a few letters in the search box. However, there are also advanced techniques that can be used, which can be helpful depending on where you're searching and what you're searching for.

Operators

One method of refining a search is to use the operators AND, OR, and NOT. These must be typed in capital letters. The table below shows how they work:

Operator	Example	Action
AND	gold AND mine	Finds files that contain both of the words "gold" and "mine".
NOT	gold NOT mine	Finds files that contain the word "gold," but not "mine".
OR	gold OR mine	Finds files that contain either of the words "gold" or "mine".

Search Filters

Search filters are a feature that find the location of files by defining specific properties, e.g. author, file size, date, etc. To use a filter, open the folder to be searched and then click in the search box. This opens the folder's search options on the toolbar as shown below:

Hot tip

Depending on where you're searching, only certain search filters are available. For example, if you're searching the Documents library, you'll see different search filters than you would in the Pictures library.

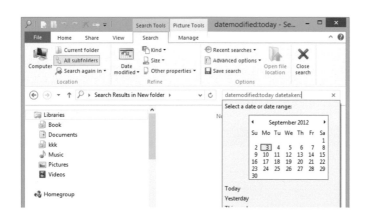

Choose the required filter and select from the available options.

You can use several filters in a search and also combine them with regular search terms to refine the search.

...cont'd

Keywords

If you cannot see the filter you need when you click in the search box, try a keyword instead. Typically, this requires a property name to be specified, then a colon, sometimes an operator, and then a value. Some examples are shown below:

Example Search Term	Action
System.FileName:~<"report"	Finds files with names beginning with "report." The ~< means "begins with"
System.FileName:="monthly report"	Finds files named "monthly report." The = means "matches exactly"
System.FileName:~="pro"	Finds files with names containing the word "pro" or the characters pro as part of another word (such as "process" or "procedure"). The ~= means "contains"
System.Kind:<>video	Finds files that aren't videos. The <> means "is not"
System.DateModified: 05/25/2013	Finds files that were modified on that date. You can also type "System. DateModified:2013" to find files changed at any time during that year
System.Author:~!"john"	Finds files whose authors don't have "john" in their name. The ~! means "doesn't contain."
System.Size:<1gb	Finds files less than 1GB in size
System.Size:>5gb	Finds files more than 5GB in size

You can also use the operators AND, OR, and NOT to combine search keywords.

Example Search Term	Action
System.Author:john AND dave	Finds files authored by John as well as files that include Dave
System.Author:john AND System.DateModified:>2013	Finds only files that are authored by John after 2013
System.Author:"john parker"	Finds files that are authored by John Parker.
System.Author:"(john* AND dave)	Files that have either John and Dave or Dave and John listed as authors.

Hot tip

In the example on the right, note how adding parentheses can change the effect of a search term.

More Right-Click Options

The right-click menu offers many useful options. Let's see how to add some more.

Move To Folder and Copy To Folder

The right-click Cut and Copy commands allow you to copy and move files to different locations. However, you have to go to the desired location to complete the operation. Here's a faster way:

1 Open the Registry Editor by going to Search in the Charms bar and typing "regedit". Then locate the following key:
HKEY_CLASSES_ROOT\AllFilesystemObjects\
shellex\ContextMenuHandlers

Both of these commands also enable you to quickly create a new folder in the desired location without having to leave the dialog box.

57

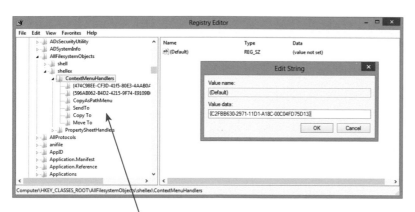

2 Right-click the ContextMenuHandlers folder and select New, Key. Name the key Copy To. Double-click the default value in the right-hand window and enter the following in the Value Data box:
{C2FBB630-2971-11D1-A18C-00C04FD75D13}

3 Repeat the above procedure, this time naming the key Move To. In the Value Data box enter the following:
{C2FBB631-2971-11D1-A18C-00C04FD75D13}

Close the Registry Editor. Now right-click a folder or file and you will see Copy To Folder and Move To Folder options.

These two commands provide a very useful means of quickly relocating data without having to go to the actual location.

...cont'd

Add Options to the Send To Menu

The Send To menu provides another very useful method of quickly relocating data. It can also be used to open a file with which an application is not associated. For example, if your image files open with Windows Photo Viewer by default, you can use the Send To feature to open an image with a different program.

If an application you would like to use in this way is not in the default Send To list, you can add it as described below:

1 The Send To folder is hidden by default. To reveal it, open Folder Options in the Control Panel and click the View tab. Then select "Show hidden files and folders"

2 Go to your C: drive, open the Users folder and click your username. Then click AppData, Roaming, Microsoft, Windows. Now you will see the Send To folder

3 In the Send To folder, create shortcuts to the applications you want to add to the Send To menu

4 When you have finished, close the folder and return to the Desktop. Your applications will now be available from the Send To menu

Hot tip

While the majority of programs work with the Send To feature, not all do. So if you try this and the program doesn't appear in the Send To list, don't waste time trying to figure out why. An example is programs from Microsoft Office Suites, such as Word, Excel and FrontPage.

58

Quick File Selection

The traditional way of selecting a bunch of files is to drag a box around them with the left mouse button depressed. Individual files are selected by holding down the Ctrl key.

Windows 8.1 provides a better way:

1 Go to Control Panel and open the Folder Options utility. Then click the View tab

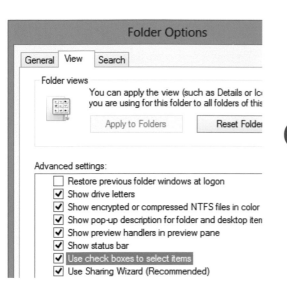

Hot tip

To deselect a number of check box-selected files, left-click once in an empty part of the folder.

2 Scroll down the list and check the "Use check boxes to select items" option

The next time you open a folder, hovering the mouse over each file opens a check box to the left of the file. Simply check the box to select the file. This method is quicker and more precise.

Hot tip

You can still select files in the traditional way by dragging a box round them.

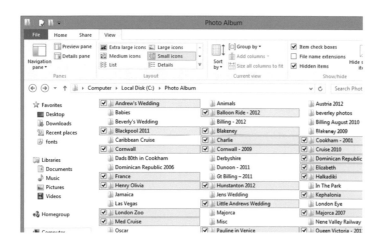

Hot tip

Use the Windows check box feature to select your files – see page 59.

Batch Renaming of Files

Have you ever been in a situation in which you have a bunch of related files with an assortment of meaningless or unrelated names? To make order of them, you have to individually rename each file, which can be a tedious task.

Well, all that is now a thing of the past. Windows 8.1 provides you with a means of sequentially renaming any number of files with the minimum of effort:

1 Select the files to be renamed

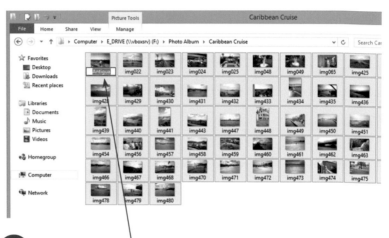

2 Right-click the first file in the list and click Rename. Type in a suitable name and then click anywhere in the folder. The files will now all be automatically renamed, as shown below:

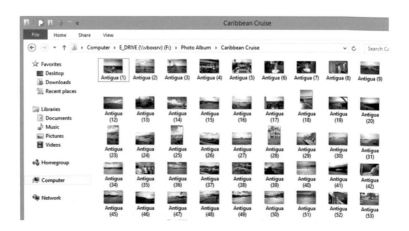

Change/Set File Associations

All files are designed to be opened with a specific type of program. For example, graphics files, such as JPEG and GIF, can only be opened by a graphics-editing program, e.g. Paint, or with a web browser, such as Internet Explorer.

A common problem that many users experience is when they install a program on their PC that automatically makes itself the default program for opening related files. If the user prefers the original program, he or she will have to reassociate the file type in question. Alternatively, the user might want to set a different program as the default:

1 Go to Control Panel, Default Programs. Click "Associate a file type or protocol with a program"

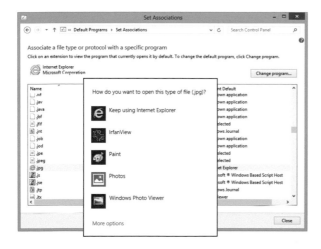

2 Select the file type and then click the Change program button

3 You will now see a list of programs on the PC capable of opening the file. Select the one you want

If a newly-installed program has rudely hijacked your favorite files, you can send it to the doghouse by reassociating the file with your favored program.

Another way is to right-click a file and then click Properties. Click the General tab and then click Change. Browse to the program you want to open the file with and select it.

Close Non-Responding Programs

Every computer user has experienced this. You close a program but instead of disappearing gracefully and without fuss, it insists on hanging around. You click the red X button repeatedly but it refuses to go.

When this happens, after a few moments a dialog box will open asking if you want to wait until the program closes or whether you want to close it yourself. The latter option will usually do the trick; however, it doesn't always work.

In this situation, do the following:

Beware

If you haven't already saved your data, closing a non-responding application with the Task Manager may result in you losing that data.

Hot tip

Every now and again, you will open a web page that causes your browser to stop responding. Use this tip to close it.

1 Right-click the taskbar and click Task Manager

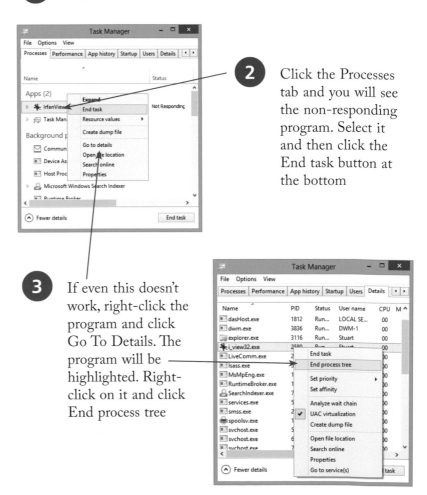

2 Click the Processes tab and you will see the non-responding program. Select it and then click the End task button at the bottom

3 If even this doesn't work, right-click the program and click Go To Details. The program will be highlighted. Right-click on it and click End process tree

Create Your Own Toolbars

Most people create shortcuts on the Desktop for frequently used programs, thus enabling them to be accessed quickly. The problem with this is that you can end up with a Desktop cluttered with many icons. Here's another way:

1 Create a folder on the Desktop and place shortcuts to the required applications in the folder. Give it a suitable name and then close it

2 Right-click the taskbar and select Toolbars, New Toolbar

Don't forget

Toolbars provide a useful means of quickly accessing your programs, and also keeping the desktop free of clutter.

63

3 Browse to the new folder and click Select Folder

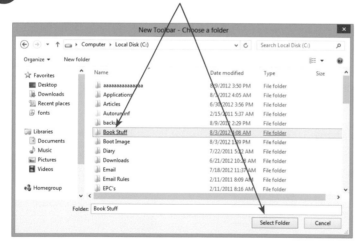

4 A toolbar containing all of your shortcuts will appear to the left of the notification area. Click the chevrons to access them

Create a Customized Control Panel

The Control Panel is a very useful and often overlooked section of Windows operating systems. From here, you can access settings that affect virtually all aspects of the computer.

It does, however, contain quite a few applications that will be of no interest to the average user: Sync Center, Credential Manager, and Speech Recognition are typical examples. There are others though, such as Internet Options, System, and Administrative Tools, that many people will use frequently.

This tip will give you quick access to the ones you use and allow you to forget about the ones you don't use:

1 Create a new folder on the desktop and name it Control Panel

2 Open the Control Panel (the real one) and create desktop shortcuts to the applications you use (right-click and select Create Shortcut)

3 Close the Control Panel and go back to the desktop. Now drag the shortcuts to the Control Panel folder

You will now have a Control Panel on the desktop that contains only the applications that you use. This will enable you to locate the items quickly instead of having to search through a long list.

Take some time to look through the Control Panel utilities. You will find a lot of Windows features and settings that you didn't know existed. Plus, you will learn a lot about your computer.

You can also use your new Control Panel folder to create a toolbar on the taskbar – see page 63.

Organize Your Data

Windows 8.1 includes a feature known as Libraries. This is a data management system that enables the user to quickly and easily organize specific types of data, e.g. images, documents, videos, etc.

The concept behind this is that of a single folder known as a Library, which contains user-defined subfolders. The subfolders are not actually stored in the library, though; they are still in their original locations. These could be a different hard drive, a flash drive or even a separate PC (in the case of a networked system). However, they are all instantly accessible from the library folder. Furthermore, any changes to the contents of the subfolders, wherever they may be, are dynamically updated in the library.

Windows starts you off with four default libraries: Music, Documents, Pictures, and Videos, which cover the main file types. These can be accessed on the navigation pane of any Explorer folder by right-clicking at the left of the folder and selecting Show libraries. Should you wish to create a new library, you can do so by clicking on Libraries, right-clicking anywhere in the Libraries folder and selecting New, Library.

To add content to a new library, open it and click Include a folder. To add content to an existing library, click Library tools at the top of the window and then Manage library.

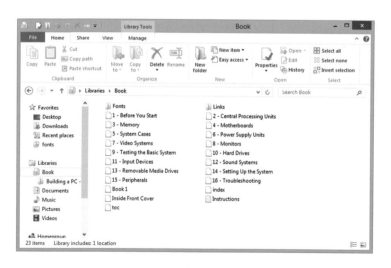

Used in conjunction, Windows Tags feature (see page 54) and Libraries provide a quick method of assimilating data and then efficiently organizing it into easily-accessible locations.

If you simply like things neat and tidy, or have a genuine need to organize your data efficiently, Windows Libraries feature is just what you need.

Windows indexes all library folders to enable fast searching.

Use Apps from Any Source

Windows 8.1 will only allow the user to install apps from trusted sources, i.e. they have to be digitally signed. This means they must be downloaded from the Windows Store – try installing an app from any other source and you won't be able to. The reasoning behind this is that it helps protect the user's security.

This is all well and good, and will indeed protect many users from themselves. However, for advanced users who are well aware of the risks and know how to deal with them, this is an unwelcome restriction that limits their use of the PC.

There is a way of circumventing this restriction, though. Do it as described below:

1 Open Search from the Charms bar and in the box type gpedit.msc

2 On the left-hand side of gpedit, click Computer Configuration, Administrative Templates, Windows Components, App Package Deployment

The gpedit.msc utility is only available on Windows 8.1 Pro and Windows 8.1 Enterprise.

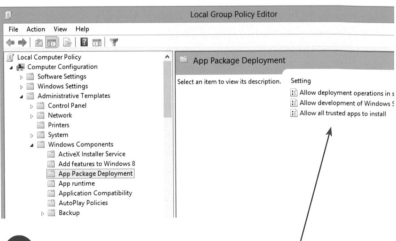

3 On the right-hand side, double-click "Allow all trusted apps to install" and then select Enabled, OK

You will now be able to install apps from any source. Just remember that you need to be careful if you don't want to end up with a virus/malware-infested computer.

Navigation Pane Folders

A very useful feature found in Windows folders is the navigation pane on the left-hand side. This displays commonly-accessed locations such as the Control Panel, Computer, Favorites, etc., and thus allows the user to navigate the computer quickly.

In Windows 8.1, however, most of these have been removed – all you get is Homegroup, This PC, and Network.

For those of you who make use of this feature, there is a way to get your frequently-used locations back.

To do this:

1 Open any Windows Explorer folder and click the View tab at the top

2 At the far-right, you'll see Options. Click the icon above Options to open the Folder Options dialog box

3 In the Navigation pane section, check "Show all folders"

For the Windows Snap feature to work, the device must have a screen width of at least 1366 pixels. If you are having problems, check this out by going to Control Panel, Display, Adjust Resolution.

Snap Your Apps

Windows apps are designed to run full-screen. With the large wide-screen monitors available today, many users will find it irritating to have their entire desktop real-estate taken up by just one program.

To address this issue, Windows 8.1 offers a feature called Snap, which enables users to run up to four apps side-by-side. The actual number depends on the monitor's resolution. Resolutions of 2,560 x 1,440 pixels can snap four apps. Resolutions less than this will only be able to snap two or three.

Here we see two apps snapped – the calendar app and the Finance app

To set this up, open the first app, which will fill the entire screen. Then hover the mouse over the top-left corner of the screen to open the Application Switcher.

Select the second app and drag it out to the left or right of the the screen depending on your requirements. When you see the black Snap bar appear, release the app and it will snap into place. If the screen's resolution allows, you can repeat this with a third or fourth app. It's as easy as that.

One way in which this feature may prove to be useful is that it enables a Windows app to be run on the classic desktop or vice versa. For example, you can use the classic desktop to do your work while simultaneously keeping an eye on your emails by having the email app snapped to one side.

Bring Back the Start Menu

Probably the most contentious change in Windows 8 was the omission of the Start menu. This feature essentially provides the way into a Windows PC and, without it, many users find it difficult to locate their programs and settings.

Fortunately, there are several third-party applications that can be downloaded from the Internet to resolve this issue. One we recommend is Classic Shell, a free download from **http://classicshell.sourceforge.net**

This program not only reinstates the Start menu but also the Start button. Both are very similar, both in appearance and function, to the original Windows versions, as shown below:

Hot tip

Another good Start menu and Start button substitute is Start8. This is available from www. stardock.com/products/ start8
You will, however, have to pay for this one.

69

Classic Shell is highly-customizable and provides many options; more so, in fact, than by Windows itself.

For example: the Start menu style, behavior, and Context menu options; not to mention different skins for both the Start menu and Start button.

It also provides options for customizing Windows Explorer and Internet Explorer.

Another feature provided by Classic Shell is options to completely bypass the Start Screen, and to disable Windows 8.1's active corners (the Charms bar, Application Switcher, etc.).

However, with Windows 8.1 Update installed, the former is no longer needed. i.e. when a computer is booted it goes directly to the Desktop. If the user wants it to boot to the Start screen, this behaviour has to be set in the taskbar options.

Miscellaneous Tips

Access an Inaccessible PC

Some programs run in full-screen mode when they are installed, thus hiding both the Desktop and Taskbar. Also, many games do the same by running permanently in full-screen mode.

If you need to open a file or program when in this situation, you can access the PC by pressing the Windows key. This opens the Start Screen; from there you can get into the PC.

Switch to Full-Screen Mode

When you're working in a folder that contains a large number of files, you can reduce the amount of scrolling necessary by simply pressing the F11 key. This switches the folder to full-screen view. Press F11 again to revert to the normal view.

Restore Previous Folders at Log On

If you log off with a bunch of folders open, Windows closes them all for you. If you want the folders to reopen in their original size and position when you log on again, do this:

1 Go to Control Panel, Folder Options. Click the View tab

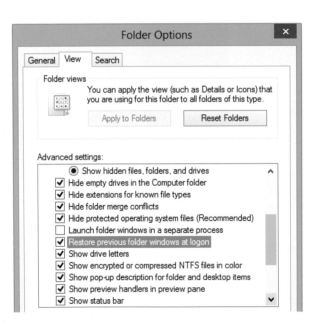

2 Check the "Restore previous folder windows at logon" box

If you want to rename a file, rather than right-clicking it and clicking Rename, select it with the mouse and then press F2.

Have you ever needed to insert the date and time in a Notepad document? Here's an easy way: rather than typing it, just press the F5 key.

Bypass the Recycle Bin

If you can live without the safety net provided by the Recycle Bin, you can speed up file deletion by doing away with it completely:

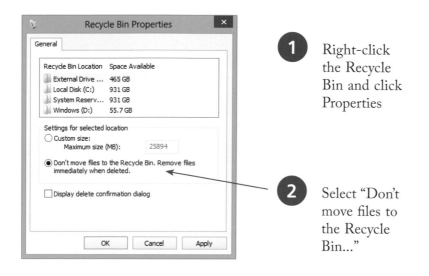

1 Right-click the Recycle Bin and click Properties

2 Select "Don't move files to the Recycle Bin..."

Another way to bypass the Recycle Bin is to hold down the Shift key as you click Delete.

Start Your Favorite Programs Automatically

This tip will enable you to start any application automatically with Windows, so it is up-and-running when the Desktop appears:

1 Press Win + R. In the Run box type:

C:\Users\username\AppData\Roaming\Microsoft\Windows\Start Menu\Programs\Startup (where username is the name of your profile folder)

2 The Startup folder will open – create shortcuts to the programs you want to auto-start. The next time you start the PC, the programs will launch automatically

When working in Windows, a quick way to undo your last action is to press Ctrl + Z.

For example: you have deleted a file by mistake. Rather than opening the Recycle Bin and searching through it, pressing Ctrl + Z will restore the file instantly.

Quick Zoom

If you want to zoom in on the contents of a folder, instead of using the Views menu, hold down the Ctrl key and scroll the mouse wheel. Move forward to zoom in and backwards to zoom out. This works in any Windows folder, on the desktop, Internet Explorer and most third-party applications.

...cont'd

Quick Search

You've got a text document open and need to find a specific word, or all instances of one. The Windows Search utility isn't much use in this situation.

Rather than read laboriously through the document, just press Ctrl + F. This opens a Find utility that will go straight to the required word and highlight it for you.

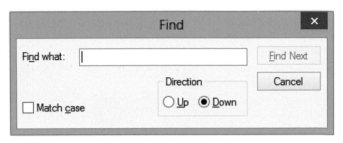

If you need to find another instance of the word, click the Find Next button

This works in any Windows text document, such as Notepad, Wordpad, and Journal. It also works in most word-processors and desktop publishing applications, all Office applications and on most web pages.

Copy as Path

Here's a handy little feature that can be a real time saver. Now and again, you need to find out the exact path of a file or folder. This could be to change a setting in the registry, or to copy a link from a network file to share into an email, etc.

The usual way of doing this is to right-click the file and click Properties. Next to Location in the General tab, you will find the file's path. Then you copy and paste it.

A much quicker way is to simply right-click the file or folder while holding the Shift key down, and click Copy as Path. Then go to your email or whatever, right-click and click Paste. Voila! Job done.

Hot tip

Internet Explorer has a similar feature called Copy Shortcut. This is also available from the right-click menu and lets you copy and paste a link as text. It is handy for inserting a link in an email, for example.

5 Things You Can Do Without

This chapter shows you how to get rid of, or moderate, some of the more irritating features in Windows 8.1. For many users, the new Windows 8.1 interface will be one of the first things to go.

User Account Control (UAC)

User Account Control is a security feature designed to protect users from themselves, i.e. unwittingly making changes to the system that can compromise its security.

The most obvious manifestations of UAC are the "Do you want to allow..." dialog boxes that pop up when the user tries to do certain actions – installing a program, for example – and the Secure Desktop (when access to the desktop is removed).

These quickly become extremely tiresome, so getting rid of UAC (or reducing its level) is probably the first thing most users will want to do. This is actually very simple as we see below:

1 Go to Control Panel, User Accounts. Click "Change User Account Control settings"

2 Drag the slider to adjust the level of UAC (bottom of the slider is off completely)

Beware

You should not disable UAC completely unless you are aware of the security issues involved. It is there for a reason.

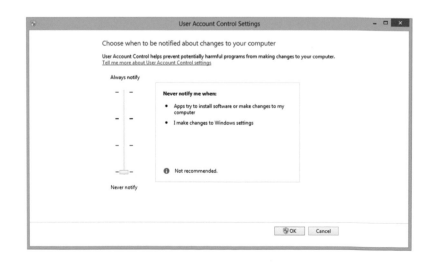

Balloon Tips

Many people find the balloon tips that regularly spring up from the notification area very irritating. Although they do sometimes give useful information, much of the time it is something obvious or that is already known to the user.

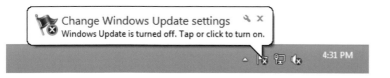

For those of you who can do without these tips, the solution is as follows:

1 Go to Control Panel, Action Center

2 Click "Change Action Center settings"

3 Remove the check marks from the notifications you don't want to receive

Balloon tips do sometimes come up with something worth knowing. For example, if your hard drive is running low on space, a balloon will pop up advising you of the fact. So you disable them at your own risk. Our recommendation is to leave them enabled.

Problem Reports

Every time an application experiences an error and is closed down by the system, Windows Problem Reporting utility will spring to life asking if you want to send details about the problem to Microsoft.

If you're the one in a million who will actually do this, then read no further. If you've no intention of complying though, you'll want to get rid of this irritation as soon as possible:

Before you disable Problem Reports, you should be aware that, if it is available, Microsoft will send you the solution to the problem. So while it is undoubtedly irritating, it can help to prevent a repeat occurrence of the problem.

1 Go to Control Panel, Action Center

2 Click Maintenance. In the new dialog box, click Settings

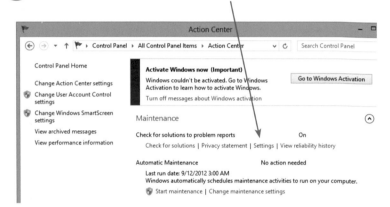

3 The Problem Reporting Settings dialog box will open. Here, you have four options, one of which is "Never check for solutions..." – this option will turn off the feature

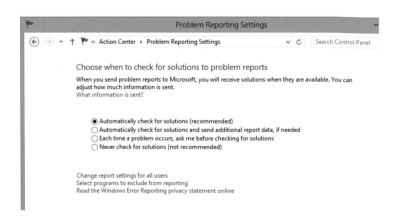

Peek

A feature introduced in Windows 7 and continued with Windows 8.1 is Peek. This is a button (invisible in Windows 8.1) located at the bottom right-hand corner of the screen. When the mouse is hovered over the button, any open windows are hidden (although their outlines remain). This is similar to the old Windows Show Desktop feature, as that is what it does – it reveals the Desktop.

While this can be useful, it can also be annoying when the cursor is moved accidentally to the button and thus hides the window you are working in.

You can disable the feature by doing the following:

In Windows 7, Peek was known as Aero Peek. In Windows 8.1, it is now just "Peek".

1 Right-click an empty area of the taskbar and click Properties

2 Remove the check from the "Use Peek to preview the desktop..." checkbox

Aero Snap

Windows 8.1 features a novel way to arrange your windows. This is known as Aero Snap and basically it provides a quick way of resizing and tiling windows.

However, like Peek, this is a feature that many users will want to disable, as at times it will cause you to resize a window when all you were intending to do was move it to a different part of the screen.

Aero Snap can be disabled as follows:

1 Go to Control Panel, Ease of Access Center

2 Click "Make the mouse easier to use"

The premise behind Aero Snap is to simplify the process of dragging and dropping between two windows, or comparing their content. Previously, this involved resizing and suitably positioning the two windows, which can take a considerable amount of mouse movement. With Aero Snap, you can grab a window and move your mouse to the edge of the screen and the window will resize to fill half the screen. Repeat with the other window. Now, with two motions, you have a setup that makes both of these scenarios much easier to accomplish.

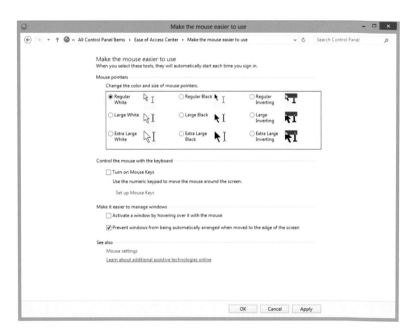

3 Check the "Prevent windows from being automatically arranged when moved to the edge of the screen" checkbox

The Aero Snap feature will no longer be active.

Lock Screen

Because Windows 8.1 can be used with touchscreens and so requires a protective barrier against accidental inputs, Microsoft has built in a lock screen. However, for users who don't have a touchscreen monitor, this is a superfluous feature.

The lock screen can be disabled as described below:

1 Right-click the Start button, select Search and type regedit. Click the regedit utility to open it

2 Using the hierarchical tree at the left navigate to: HKEY_LOCAL_MACHINE\SOFTWARE\Policies\ Microsoft\Windows

3 Right-click on the Windows folder and select New, Key. Right-click the key, select Rename and name it Personalization

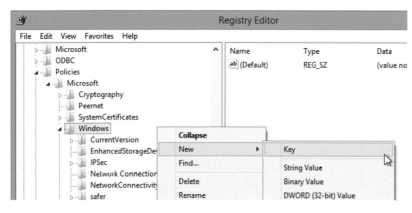

4 Right-click on the Personalization folder and select New, DWORD (32-bit) Value. Name the key NoLockScreen

5 Double-click the NoLockScreen key and in the Value data box enter a value of 1

Should you wish to reinstate the lock screen at some point, change the Value data box to read 0.

Close the registry editor. The new setting will take effect immediately. The next time you reboot or wake your computer you won't see the lock screen. Instead you'll go straight to the Windows sign in screen.

AutoPlay

AutoPlay is one of those Windows features that attempts to be helpful by providing related options that the user may not know how to access. Whenever removable media (DVDs, external hard drives, USB flash drives, etc.) are connected to the PC, a dialog box opens offering options that Windows thinks is relevant to the content on the media.

Many users, however, have no need for AutoPlay and find it is more of a nuisance than anything else. It can be disabled, or modified, as follows:

Hot tip

AutoPlay has long been regarded as an unsecure feature that provides an entry point for viruses. The version supplied with Windows 8.1 is much more secure.

1 Go to the Control Panel and open AutoPlay

2 To disable AutoPlay completely, uncheck "Use AutoPlay for all media and devices"

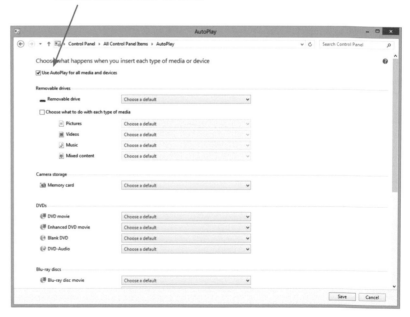

If you find the feature useful for certain types of media, you can modify the way AutoPlay behaves when media of that type is connected to the PC.

Just click the relevant drop-down box and select a suitable option.

The Windows 8.1 Interface

Windows 8.1 is presented in such a way that it is very difficult to avoid the Start screen. This is annoying for the many users who run large-screen desktop PCs with a non-touchscreen monitor.

They have little or no use for the Start screen, and will instead much prefer their PC to boot directly to the classic Desktop so they don't have to click through the Windows 8.1 interface to get to where they want to be.

This issue can be resolved as follows:

 On the Windows Desktop, right-click on the taskbar and select Properties. Click the Navigation tab

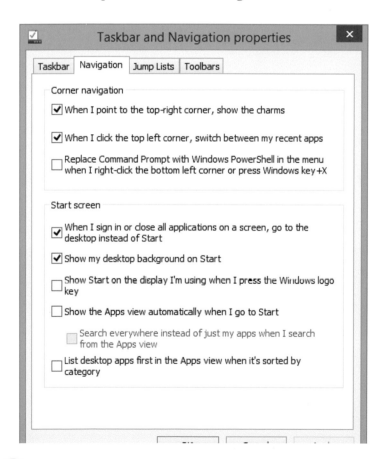

2 Under Start screen, check the "Go to the desktop instead of Start when I sign in" checkbox

Log On Password

By default, every time a Windows 8.1 PC is started, a password has to be entered before the Start screen opens. However, for the many users who don't require the security provided by password protection, not only is this a nuisance, it also slows down the startup procedure unnecessarily.

To get rid of the requirement to log on:

1 Open Search from the Charms bar. Type "netplwiz" and press Enter. The following window will open:

2 Uncheck the "Users must enter a user name and password to use this computer" checkbox. In the next dialog box, enter the current logon password and click OK

The next time you start the computer, Windows will log you on automatically.

6 Customization

There are many ways to change the default appearance of Windows 8.1 in order to personalize the PC. This chapter shows you the most common ones, plus some others that are not so well known.

The Windows Interface

Customizing the appearance of Windows allows you to create a computing environment in which you feel comfortable. Windows 8.1 gives you two interfaces to adjust to your liking – the Windows 8.1 interface and the Classic Windows interface.

Windows 8.1 Interface

In keeping with the rationale behind Windows 8.1, this offers few customizing options. The only things you can alter are the Lock screen, the Start screen background and your account picture:

1 Open the Charms bar from the Start screen and click Settings. Then click Personalize at the top of the window. You'll now see options that allow you to choose from a number of preconfigured Start screen backgrounds, or specify a solid color

2 Next, go back to the Charms bar and select Settings, Change PC settings. You will see three options – Lock screen, Account picture and Picture password

Hot tip

Configuration options for Notifications are restricted to a simple On or Off.

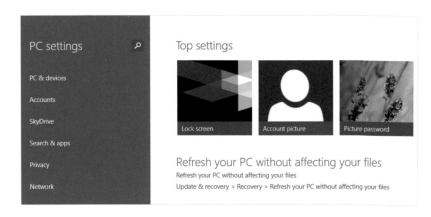

The Lock screen option allows you to select a preconfigured background or to choose one of your own pictures. You can also specify which apps you want to place notifications on the lock screen.

The Account picture option allows you to browse the PC to choose your own picture.

The final option, Picture password is a security feature which is not relevant here.

Classic Windows Interface

Right-click on the Windows Desktop and select Personalize. The Personalization dialog box will open:

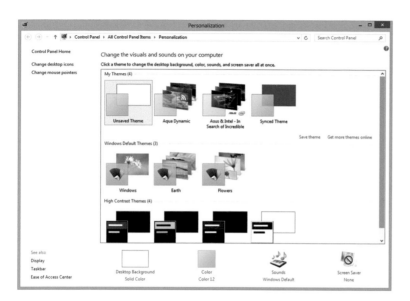

Here you have options to customize the Desktop background, sounds, screensavers, window borders and the Taskbar.
For example, to customize the latter:

1 Click Color at the bottom of the Window

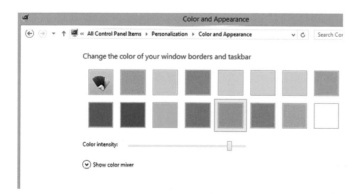

2 Choose from a range of preset colors. If you don't like any of the presets, use the color mixer to get the exact color you want. You can also adjust the color intensity

...cont'd

The Start screen offers few customizing options, as we have already explained on page 84. The Windows Desktop, however, provides much more. Here, you have four main things to look at:

Size (Resolution)

The first is the Desktop's resolution. If it's too high, the Desktop will be too small, i.e. it won't stretch to the full width and depth of the monitor, plus the icons and icon text will be too small. If it's too low, the Desktop will be too big and everything will be chunky and blocky.

Common resolution settings are:

- 17- and 19-inch monitors – 1280 x 1024

- 20- and 21-inch monitors – 1600 x 1200

- 23-inch monitors – 1920 x 1200

Check this out as follows:

1   Right-click the Desktop and click Screen Resolution

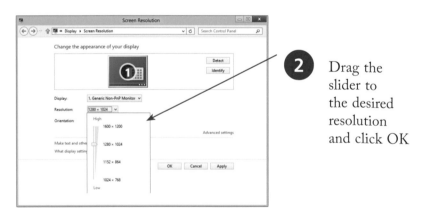

2 Drag the slider to the desired resolution and click OK

Icon Size

If you don't like the default size of the Desktop icons, there are two ways to change them:

- Right-click the Desktop and select View. Then choose from three preset options: large, medium or small.

- Hold down the Ctrl key and scroll the mouse wheel. This will enable you to set the icons size more precisely.

Hot tip

While you have the Screen Resolution dialog box open, check that your refresh rate is correct. Click Advanced Settings and then the Monitor tab. Under Screen Refresh Rate, select the highest setting available from the drop-down box.

Background

Now, turn your attention to the background – it's a fair bet that you won't want to keep the default image. Select your own by right-clicking the desktop and clicking Personalize. Then click Desktop Background – choose either an image or a color.

Select Windows Desktop Backgrounds from the drop-down box, make your selection and click Save Changes

If you don't like any of Windows' wallpapers, it's a simple matter to make your own. All you need to know is where to put them. Windows' Wallpaper folder is located in the Windows folder on the C: drive. Open it and scroll down to the Web folder. Inside this is the Wallpaper folder. Place your images here and Windows will resize them automatically when they are selected.

Text

The final thing you may want to change is the size of the text used by Windows in various places.

 1 Right-click the Desktop and click Personalize. Then click Display. Under "Change only the text size" select an item from the drop-down box and the required text size

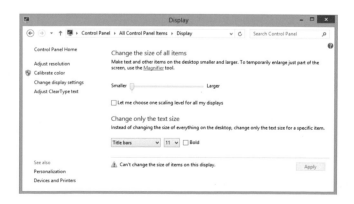

Image proportions should be similar to those of Windows wallpapers (4 x 3). Otherwise, some of it will be cropped out during the resizing.

Create your own Theme

Getting Windows looking just like you want it to can take some time. Unfortunately, if you subsequently change it, either by accident or design, you'll never be able to recreate it exactly.

There is, however, an easy way round this. Windows allows you to save your theme settings so you can get them back with a single mouse click:

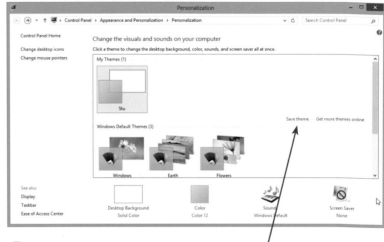

Hot tip

To create a shared theme, simply right-click a theme and then click "Save theme for sharing". The theme will be saved with a .themepack file format that can be applied on another computer running Windows 8.1.

1 Having created your theme, click "Save theme"

2 Give your theme a name

At the top of the Personalization utility window, under My Themes, your new theme will be listed. Just click to select it. You can create and save any number of themes.

Another option provided by Windows enables you to share the themes you create, or use those created by others. For example, a theme can be uploaded to a website, from where it can be downloaded by other users. Or you can save it on removable media and load it on to another PC.

Get More Windows Themes

Windows 8.1 provides little in the way of themes and what there is, is essentially just variations of the same basic theme.

If you want more, your only option is to fire-up your browser and head off into cyberspace. Here, you will discover that there is a virtually limitless number of themes, or "skins" as they are often called, available for download.

These come in an infinite range of colors and styles and will enable you to radically change the way Windows looks. The illustrations below show two (rather extreme) examples:

Hot tip

If you're interested in themes, visit **www. wincustomize.com** Here, you will find hundreds of categorized themes for Windows.

Beware

Some of the themes available on the Internet can contain bugs and thus cause instability problems on the PC.

The Taskbar

The Taskbar is a highly configurable part of Windows and setting it up to suit your method of working is important. There are quite a few adjustments you can make here that are not obvious at first glance.

Taskbar Size and Position

The first thing you might want to change is the size of the Taskbar. The default setting looks like this:

By right-clicking the Taskbar and selecting Properties, you will see that there is a "Use small taskbar buttons" option. Select this to decrease the depth of the Taskbar, as shown below:

You can also resize the Taskbar to any depth you require by right-clicking and de-selecting "Lock the taskbar". Then, hold the cursor over the top edge of the Taskbar and you will be able to drag it to the depth you want. Then relock it. However, this can look a bit odd as the icons are placed at the top, as shown below:

You can get round this by docking the Taskbar at the right or left of the screen. Here, we see it docked at the right:

Hot tip

If you want to change the order of a Taskbar icon, simply drag it to the required position. This also applies to icons in the notification area.

Hot tip

Right-clicking a Taskbar icon reveals a jump list of recent files associated with the application. You can also access the jump list by left-clicking an icon and dragging upwards at the same time.

Do this by unlocking it as previously described and simply dragging it to the required location. Increasing the size of the Taskbar and having it docked at the side of the screen is an ideal way of making use of the extra screen real-estate provided by modern wide-screen monitors.

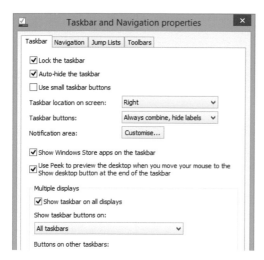

If you need as much screen space as possible, you can also auto-hide the Taskbar so that it releases the space it occupies when not being accessed. Do this by right-clicking the Taskbar and selecting Properties. Then check "Auto-hide the taskbar".

While you have the Taskbar properties dialog box open, you can also set how icons are displayed on the Taskbar. The default is "Always combine, hide labels", whereby files of the same type are all represented by one Taskbar icon as shown below:

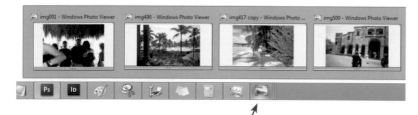

Hovering the cursor over the icon reveals a thumbnail of each file. One advantage of this is that all the files can be closed with one click.

If you choose the "Never combine" option, grouping is turned off and all files will have an individual Taskbar icon. The icons will also be larger, which can be useful for some users. The disadvantage is that each file has to be closed individually.

System Icons

Windows comes with a set of system icons. These won't be to everyone's taste though, so fortunately it's an easy task to change them to something more to your liking.

To change the icon of a system folder, such as This PC or the Recycle Bin, you first have to create a shortcut to it. To demonstrate this we will change the icon for the Recycle Bin:

Hot tip

If you can't find an icon that appeals, there are literally thousands available on the Internet. To associate downloaded icons with a program, in Step 3 use the Browse button to find and select the icon.

92

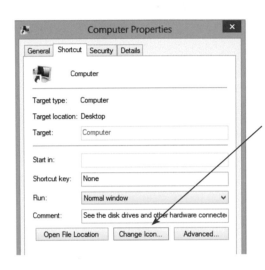

1 Right-click the Recycle Bin icon and click Create Shortcut

2 Right-click the shortcut, click Properties and then Change Icon. This will open an icon folder

3 Make a selection and then click OK

Now all you need to do is delete the original Recycle Bin icon. This procedure will work with most system folders. It will also work with third-party applications, most of which will come with an icon folder of their own (these will open instead of the icon folder shown above).

Folder Icons

Quite apart from changing icons for system folders and third-party applications, Windows allows you to change (and also customize) individual folder icons.

Do this as follows:

1 Right-click inside the folder you want to customize and then click "Customize this folder"

Hot tip

Picture icons are an alternative way of identifying the contents of a folder.

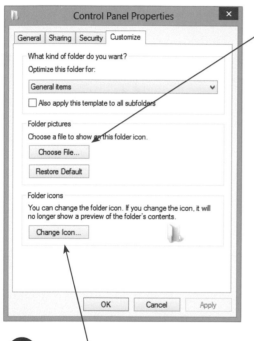

2 To customize the folder with an image, click "Choose File" and then browse to your desired picture

3 The image will be inserted into the folder icon as shown below

4 To change the folder's icon, click Change Icon. Then browse to an icon folder and make your choice

Don't forget

You may need to select a larger icon size in order to see the image placed in a folder.

Note that if you place a folder customized in this way on the desktop, you may need to select a larger icon size to see the picture.

Using pictures is a useful way of personalizing folders, and also provides another method of identifying their contents.

Display a Log On Message

In certain situations, it can be useful to greet users of a computer with a message when they log on. This might be something friendly or a warning of some description. An example of the latter could occur in an office environment where it is common for company email and Internet facilities to be misused by employees:

Hot tip

To access the Registry Editor, press Win + R and type regedit in the Run box.

1 Open the Registry Editor and locate the following key: HKEY_LOCAL_MACHINE\SOFTWARE\Microsoft\ Windows NT\CurrentVersion\Winlogon

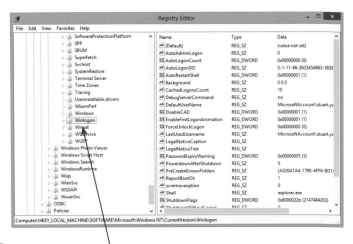

2 Click the Winlogon folder, and in the right-hand window double-click LegalNoticeCaption. In the Value Data box, type your caption, e.g. ATTENTION

Hot tip

This feature is really intended for system administrators. However, you may find a use for it.

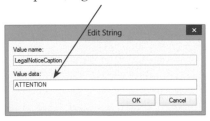

3 Click LegalNoticeText. In the Value Data box, type the message to be displayed

Reboot the computer and your captioned message will be displayed before the Lock screen appears.

7 Paranoia

There are any number of reasons why a user might want to keep his/her activities private, both on the PC and the Internet. This chapter looks at the ways that users unwittingly reveal what they've been doing and shows how to avoid them. We also look at security on the Internet.

Keep your Activities Private

It's not easy to use a computer without leaving traces of what you have been doing. Windows keeps records of user activity in several places, and anyone who knows where to look can find out what websites you've visited, files you've accessed, programs you've been using, etc. If you're not careful, they can even access your password-protected web pages.

The following are the most common giveaways:

Jump Lists

When you right-click a program's icon on the taskbar, a Jump List of files recently opened with that program will be revealed, as shown below.

If you have been using Microsoft Word to type a letter to your Bank Manager, for example, a subsequent user will be able to see the name of the file in the Jump List and also open it. To prevent this, do the following:

1 Right-click the Taskbar and click Properties. Then click the Jump Lists tab

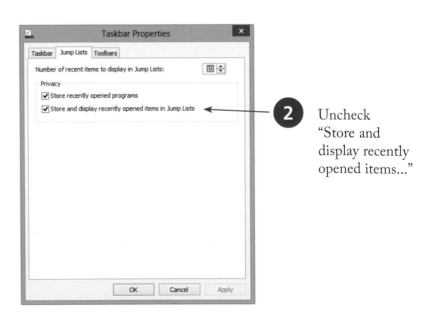

Hot tip

Note that this action will disable the Jump list feature completely. It will still be there but with no items on it.

2 Uncheck "Store and display recently opened items…"

Hot tip

Items in Jump Lists can be deleted individually by right-clicking and then clicking "Remove from this list". However, one day you will forget to do it. This tip provides a permanent solution so you don't have to keep checking that you've done it.

96

Most Recently Used Lists (MRUs)

The most common method of preventing other users from seeing a private file is to simply squirrel it away in a location that is not likely to be accessed by someone else – out of sight, out of mind, as the saying goes.

However, while a file hidden in this way may be difficult to physically locate, there is a way for another user to easily find it.

This is courtesy of the Most Recently Used files feature, found in most programs, that enables a user to reopen a recent file quickly without having to go to its location.

So a user looking to keep a particular file private will need to clear the MRU list in any program it has been accessed with recently – see margin note.

Windows Searches

Another method of finding data is using the Windows Search utility. No matter how well a user hides a file, if another user specifies that file type in a search, the file will be revealed.

For example, if someone was to type .doc into the search box all Microsoft Word documents would be found.

The problem here is that there is no way to configure the Search utility to prevent another user from searching for a file of a specific type.

Hot tip

With most programs, the MRU list can be cleared by disabling the feature. The option for doing this is usually found in the Options menu.

...cont'd

So the only way to prevent files being revealed by Windows searches is to place them in a password-protected folder.

Unfortunately, Windows 8.1 does not provide a way to password-protect individual folders. The only way to do it, therefore, is to install a third-party utility – see page 111.

Run Command History

The Run command (accessed by pressing Win + R) keeps a history of all entries made. This can reveal to other users what files, and even web pages, you have accessed.

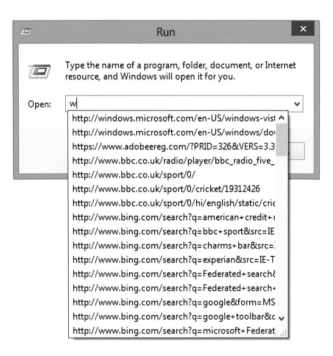

For example, someone typing the letter W into the Run box will see a list of all the web pages that have been accessed since the history folder was last cleared. Furthermore, by selecting an entry and clicking OK, the web page will be opened in the PC's browser.

There is a registry setting that will clear the Run history, but an easier way is to download and install a program called MRU-Blaster from **www.brightfort.com**
This is a free utility that will clear not only the Windows Run History but also program MRUs (see page 97).

Hide your Browsing Tracks

Browsing History

In the same way that Windows keeps records of user activity, so does Internet Explorer.

This information is held in the following places:

- **History Folder** – this folder holds a chronological record of every website and page visited

- **Temporary Internet Files Folder** – this folder is a cache of the pages you have accessed. Should you revisit a particular web page, your browser will retrieve it from this cache rather than from the Web. This makes access to the page quicker

- **Cookies Folder** – cookies are text files that websites download to your PC. They have several purposes; one is to identify you should you visit that website again. Often, they will also reveal the type of website, e.g. stuart@luckydollarcasino

For users who wish to keep their Internet activities private, Internet Explorer provides a Delete Browsing History utility. To access it, open Internet Explorer, click the Tools button and then "Delete Browsing History".

Don't forget to check your Internet Favorites. When accessed, certain websites will automatically place a link to their website here. Common culprits in this respect are porn and gambling websites. Anyone who happens to use your browser may see anything which has been added in this way.

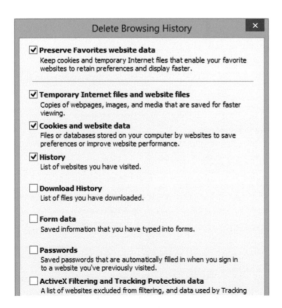

The utility enables you to eradicate all records of your Internet activities, or just some of them by clicking the Settings button.

…cont'd

AutoComplete

Internet Explorer has a feature called AutoComplete that enables the browser to automatically enter web addresses, usernames, passwords and data entered on web-based forms. This can be convenient as it saves the user from having to type out this information each time.

However, it can also be dangerous as it allows other people to access your password-protected pages, and see what data you've entered in forms, etc. It will also enable any snooper to see which websites you have visited, and any keywords entered in search engine search boxes.

If you wish to keep this type of information private then you need to disable AutoComplete or alter its settings:

The safest way to use AutoComplete is to disable the "User names and passwords on forms" option. Enabling it to remember web addresses is safe and can be very useful.

1 Go to Control Panel, Internet Options. Click the Content tab

2 Click Settings in the AutoComplete section

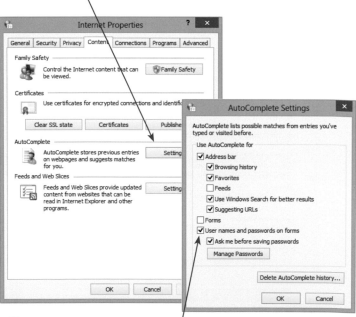

Disabling any of AutoComplete's settings will also remove any information previously held regarding the setting. It won't still be there should you subsequently re-enable it.

3 Remove the checks from "Address Bar" and "User names and passwords on forms"

InPrivate Browsing

As we have seen on page 99, it is possible to delete your browsing history after the session. However, there are two problems with this approach:

- You may forget to do it

- You have to delete the entire history when maybe all you want to do is to delete a small part of it – it's an all-or-nothing action

The solution is a feature in Internet Explorer called InPrivate Browsing. When used, InPrivate temporarily suspends Internet Explorer's automatic caching functions and, at the same time, keeps your previous browsing history intact. A typical example of when you might want to do this is buying a gift online for a loved one; once done, you can revert to browsing as normal. Your browsing history up to the point of opening the InPrivate session is kept but the InPrivate session itself is not.

There are two ways of opening an InPrivate session:

 In Internet Explorer, click Tools on the menu bar and select InPrivate Browsing

Note that, by default, the menu bar in Internet Explorer is disabled. Enable it by right-clicking at the top of a Internet Explorer window and selecting Menu bar.

While InPrivate Browsing keeps other people who use your computer from seeing what sites you've visited, it does not prevent someone on your network, such as a network administrator.

If you don't see the menu bar, right-click at the top of a Internet Explorer window and select Menu bar.

...**cont'd**

2 Right-click Internet Explorer on the taskbar and select Start InPrivate Browsing. This opens an InPrivate session

InPrivate Browsing does not provide you with anonymity on the Internet. For example, websites might be able to identify you through your web address. Also, anything you do on a website can be recorded by that website.

A handy tip for those who will do a lot of InPrivate browsing is to configure Internet Explorer to open InPrivate by default. Do this as follows:

1 Right-click on the desktop and select New, Shortcut

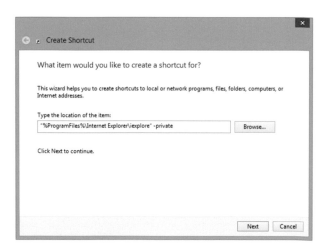

2 In the "Location of the item" box, type:
"%ProgramFiles%\Internet Explorer\iexplore" -private
Click Next, name the shortcut Internet Explorer and then replace the original Internet Explorer icon with the new one

Anonymous Browsing

Personal privacy on the Internet, as any computer-savvy user knows, is becoming increasingly difficult to maintain. In many cases, the content you view actually comes from third-party sites. While most of these sites are quite legitimate, there are some who conceal scripts in their content that track your actions as you browse the Internet.

To help protect users against this, Windows 8.1 offers a feature known as Tracking Protection. This enables you to prevent specific third-party sites from tracking your online movements.

The system works by loading tracking protection lists (TPLs) of known offenders into Internet Explorer. As you subsequently browse the Internet, Internet Explorer will prevent your data from being accessed by any of the sites specified in the TPLs:

1 You can add a tracking protection list by clicking the Tools icon at the top far-right of Internet Explorer. Then click Safety, Turn on Tracking Protection

2 Click "Get a Tracking Protection List online". This opens a website that provides TPLs from various sources

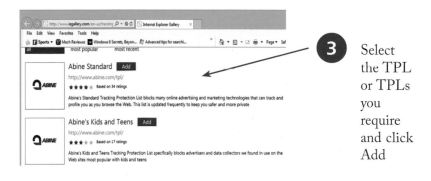

3 Select the TPL or TPLs you require and click Add

...cont'd

The TPL will now be added to Internet Explorer. At this point, you may wish to see what sites are included in the list and, if necessary, edit the list.

Beware

Internet Explorer automatically generates a TPL based on the sites the user visits. This is called "Your Personalized List", and is in addition to any TPLs added by the user.

4 Open Manage Add-ons as described in Step 1. You will now see the TPLs you have installed

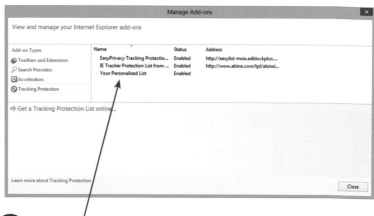

5 Double-click an entry to open the TPL personalization dialog box as shown below

6 You will now see each website on the list. Right-clicking on an entry provides options to allow or block the website

Hide your Drives

The following procedure does more than just hide a file or folder – it actually hides the drive where the file/folder is located:

1 Start the Registry Editor and locate the following key: HKEY_CURRENT_USER\Software\Microsoft\ Windows\CurrentVersion\Policies

2 Right-click the Policies folder and click New, Key. Name the new key Explorer

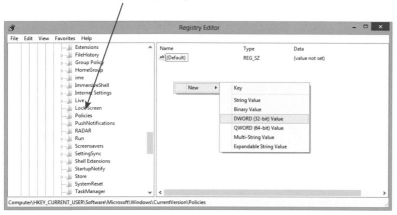

3 Click the Explorer folder and on the right, right-click and select New, DWORD. Name it NoDrives. Right-click NoDrives and in the Value Data box, enter the number of the drive (shown in the table below) to be hidden

Drive A – 1	Drive J – 512	Drive S – 262144
Drive B – 2	Drive K – 1024	Drive T – 524288
Drive C – 4	Drive L – 2048	Drive U – 1048576
Drive D – 8	Drive M – 4096	Drive V – 2097152
Drive E – 16	Drive N – 8192	Drive W – 4194304
Drive F – 32	Drive O – 16384	Drive X – 8388608
Drive G – 64	Drive P – 32768	Drive Y – 16777216
Drive H – 128	Drive Q – 65536	Drive Z – 33554432
Drive I – 256	Drive R – 131072	All – 67108863

Hot tip

To unhide a drive, enter 0 in the Value Data box. Now, if you are going to be hiding and unhiding a drive on a regular basis, having to go into the registry each time will be a pain. So instead, you can create a shortcut.

Create a NoDrives DWORD, as described, and give it a value of 0. Then right-click the Explorer folder on the left and click Export. In the File Name box, type: Unhide.reg. Then save it to the desktop.

Next, go back to the NoDrives DWORD and in the Value Data box enter the number of the drive to be hidden. Return to the Explorer folder and export it as described above, this time with the name Hide.reg.

Now just click the Hide icon to conceal the drive and the Unhide icon to reveal it (not forgetting to reboot).

Another way to hide a folder is to simply squirrel it away in a folder containing a mass of other folders or sub-folders. Just don't forget which one you put it in.

The method described on this page, while useful, is by no means secure. Anyone who knows about this feature will be able to access anything you hide in this way.

Hide your Private Files

Users who want to hide a file or folder quickly can do so by means of Windows Hidden Files and Folders feature. While this is intended primarily to conceal important system files, which if modified or deleted can cause damage to the operating system, it can also be used to hide other files or folders.

1 Right-click the file to be hidden and click Properties

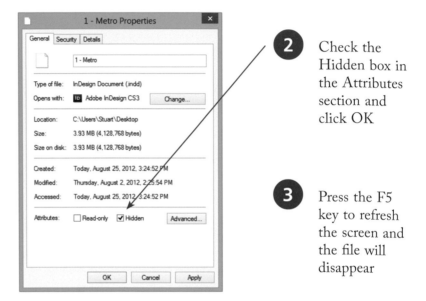

2 Check the Hidden box in the Attributes section and click OK

3 Press the F5 key to refresh the screen and the file will disappear

4 To unhide the file, go to Folder Options in the Control Panel. Click the View tab, and check "Show hidden files, folders, and drives"

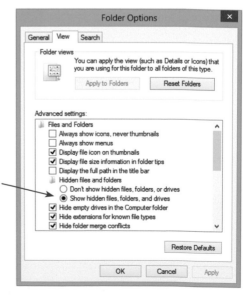

8 Security

Most laptops provide a connector to which a cable can be connected to secure them.

Locking devices for removable media drives are also available. These are mounted on the front panel of the drive and prevent access to it.

Secure your PC Physically

One of the most glaring security loopholes of all is physical theft. The PC's data may be well secured but what's to prevent someone from simply tucking the system case under their arm and walking away with it. They may not be able to access the data on the PC but you've still lost it.

While your home insurance (if you have it – many don't, and assuming it pays out) will cover the cost of replacing the PC, it won't replace your data.

So if yours is irreplaceable, and you are not in the habit of creating up-to-date backups on separate media (writable discs, USB flash drives, etc), or cannot afford to be without the PC for the length of time needed to replace it, then you need to physically secure it.

The following methods are available:

Alarms
These are the least effective method as they don't provide any physical restraint, but may be sufficient to deter the casual thief. A typical system will consist of a motion sensor that you fix to the system case. If someone tries to open the case or pick it up, an alarm will be triggered.

Cables
A cable system consists of plates, which are fixed to the case and peripherals by bolts or industrial-strength adhesive. The cable is fixed to one plate, looped through the others and then fixed to an anchor plate on the desk. To steal the PC, the thief will have to steal the desk along with it. They can, however, open the case and steal all the components inside.

Enclosures
These are lockable heavy-duty metal boxes into which the system case is placed, and are secured to the desk by bolts or adhesive. This is the best method as not only is it impossible to steal the PC, it is also impossible to open the case and steal the PC's components.

So, if you want to keep both the PC and the data it contains safe, take steps to physically secure it.

Restrict Access to Windows

The next step is to prevent access to the operating system. Here are three ways to do this:

Set a Boot Password

Most BIOS setup programs provide an option to password-protect the bootup procedure. To do this, start the PC and enter the BIOS setup program – see page 125.

On the opening screen you should see an option to "Set User Password". Select this and enter a password; this password-protects the BIOS setup program. Then, look for a security option (usually found in the Advanced BIOS Features page). This enables you to set a boot password. Do so, save the changes and exit the BIOS. Now bootup will stop at the boot screen and ask you to enter the password.

Set a Log On Password

During the installation routine of Windows 8.1, the user is asked to specify a password. However, this is only mandatory if using a Microsoft account; if you set up Windows using a local account, a password is not necessary.

If the latter option was taken when the PC was set up, you can set a password now as described below:

Password-protecting the BIOS setup program as well, means a hacker has two passwords to crack before the PC can be booted-up.

1 Press Win + C to open the Charms bar. Click Settings, Change PC settings, and Accounts. Then click Sign-in options

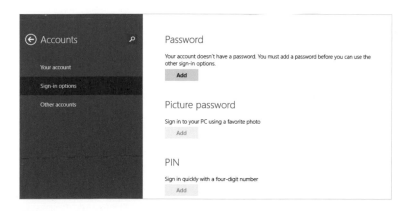

2 Under Password, click Add. Then follow the prompts to create a log on password

109

...cont'd

Create an Encrypted Password Disk

This is an extremely secure method of securing a PC by using an encrypted key. Read the margin note before you get started.

<u>WARNING</u>: The procedure cannot be undone. Be quite sure that you need this level of security before you start.

1 Open Run by pressing Win + R, enter syskey in the box and press Enter

The syskey utility requires a floppy disk as the storage medium. However, very few PCs use floppy drives these days so a better option is to use a USB flash drive. This will need to be configured to use the A: drive letter commonly assigned to the floppy drive.

This can be done in Windows Drive Management, which is located in the Control Panel. Click Administrative Tools, Computer Management, Disk Management. Right-click the USB drive and select "Change drive letter and paths...".

Note that if the A: drive letter is not available, you will need to disable the floppy drive in the PC's BIOS.

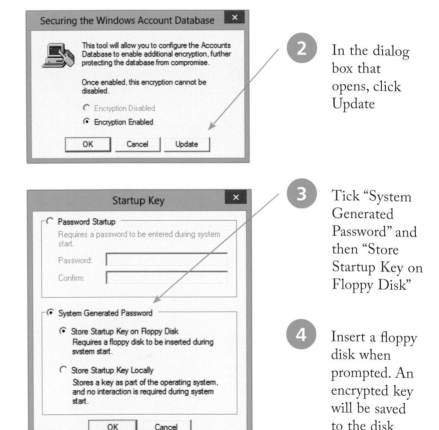

2 In the dialog box that opens, click Update

3 Tick "System Generated Password" and then "Store Startup Key on Floppy Disk"

4 Insert a floppy disk when prompted. An encrypted key will be saved to the disk

From this point on, every time you boot the PC, it will be necessary to insert the disk into the floppy drive before you can access the log on screen. So just make sure you don't lose it, otherwise you won't be able to access your own computer.

Password-Protect Folders

With access to both the PC and the operating system secured, the really security-conscious user may want to make things even more difficult for a potential intruder. The way to do this is to password-protect any sensitive data so that even if someone does manage to gain entry to the PC, they can't get to your data.

Unfortunately, Windows 8.1 doesn't provide a folder/file password-protection function. The only option therefore, is to use a third-party application. Do a Google search and you will find dozens of programs of this type. A typical example is one called Folder Password Protect, which is available from **www.protect-folders.com**

This simple but effective application lets you password-protect any number of folders, either individually or collectively, by adding them to a main window, as shown below:

A badly-written password-protection utility can be more dangerous than not having one at all. If it contains bugs, you could well end up losing your passwords and thus your data. For this reason, give freeware and shareware programs a definite miss.

111

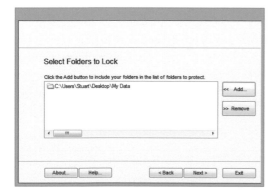

When the files to be protected have been added, click Next, and in the new dialog box enter the desired password. Click OK and you're done – the selected folder, or folders, are protected.

To unprotect a folder, select it and enter the password. It couldn't be simpler.

Keep your Passwords Safe

Most computer users these days will have several passwords – many will have a dozen or more. It can be difficult to remember these passwords, particularly those that are rarely used. Accordingly, many users keep a file on the PC that contains all their passwords.

However, while this ensures they don't forget them, a new problem arises – password theft. Unfortunately, Windows does not provide a utility that can be used to safely store and manage passwords.

So what we suggest is that you acquire a Password Manager program. The easiest way is to download one from the Internet; you will find literally hundreds – some free, some not. The one shown below, Password Manager, is a typical example.

These programs work by hiding the passwords behind asterisks; a mouse click is required to reveal them. Thus, malicious software will not be able to see what they are. The password managers themselves are also password-protected to prevent physical access by a snooper. So all you have to do is remember a single password.

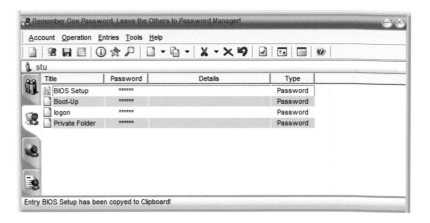

Good password managers have an auto-fill facility, similar to Internet Explorer's AutoComplete. It should also be possible to install and run them from removable media. A good example is RoboForm, which can be used from a flash drive.

Encrypt your Private Data

We've seen how to secure your data by password-protecting both it and the PC. What we haven't considered yet is the possibility of someone cracking your password. The answer to this is to encrypt the data itself, thus adding a further layer of protection.

Windows 8.1 provides data encryption via its Encrypting File System (EFS) feature and it's very easy to use. Simply right-click the folder containing files to be encrypted and click Properties. Then click the Advanced button and in the dialog box that opens, select "Encrypt contents to secure data". When the encryption has finished, the names of the encrypted files will change to green signifying that they are encrypted.

However, even though it is encrypted, the data is still vulnerable to someone who either physically steals the entire PC, or the drive the data is stored on. This is due to the fact that EFS only works on drives formatted with the NTFS file system, so if the encrypted folder is copied to a non-NTFS drive, the encryption is removed and the data will thus be accessible.

To guard against this, you need to use another feature provided by Windows 8.1. This is called BitLocker Drive Encryption and it provides "offline" data protection by making it possible to encrypt an entire drive (including removable USB flash drives).

Go to Control Panel and click BitLocker Drive Encryption. Click "Turn On BitLocker" next to the drive to be encrypted and then follow the prompts – this will include setting a password to unlock the drive. Note that the encryption process can take a very long time. When it is finished, if you go to This PC, you will see that the encrypted drive now has a padlocked drive icon.

If you remove the drive and then re-install it, a dialog box will pop up asking for the password, as shown on the left.

To remove encryption or set a different method of unlocking the drive, re-open the utility and select "Manage BitLocker".

Data Backup

The final way in which your data can be compromised is losing it. This can be accidental deletion, a virus attack, hardware or operating system failure, or data corruption. As a safeguard against any of these potential threats, you need to create a backup on a separate medium.

Traditionally, this has required a backup program and Windows 8 provided an excellent imaging utility that was called Windows 7 File Recovery. However, in Windows 8.1 it has been removed, and the reason is that Microsoft are pushing the Cloud as a backup medium via its OneDrive app.

Therefore, anyone wishing to do image or large-scale backups in Windows 8.1 will have to purchase a third-party utility. There are many good choices here and one we can recommend is Acronis True Image. This offers image backups, continuous backups in real time plus a host of other features.

Windows itself offers just two methods of data backup: File History, which we look at on page 115, and the afore-mentioned OneDrive app. The latter is deeply integrated in Windows 8.1, which makes it very straightforward to use.

For example, when you save a document with the Save As command, the first option you see is OneDrive. Select this and the file will be seamlessly uploaded to your OneDrive account where it will be safe from whatever catastrophe may befall your PC.

Furthermore, by default, your Documents folder is synced to your online OneDrive account. So files can be automatically backed up simply by placing them in the Documents folder.

Thus, OneDrive provides an ideal method of backing up small files. The drawbacks are that the maximum file size that can be uploaded is currently 300MB, and that the total amount of free storage is restricted to just 7GB (*at the time of printing*). If you need more you will have to pay for it.

Configure your OneDrive settings by going to the Charms bar and selecting Settings, Change PC settings. Then click OneDrive. Here you will be able to monitor your storage space, and specify folders and settings to be automatically backed up online.

For those of you not up to speed with current computer terminology, "the cloud" or "cloud computing" is a term for the delivery of hosted services over the Internet. On this page it refers to the use of the free storage space provided by Microsoft, which users can use to safely store their data via the OneDrive app.

A big advantage of using OneDrive to back up your data is that once configured the process is automatic – you'll never forget to do it.

Recover your Data

File History is a replacement for the Previous Versions utility found in Windows Vista and Windows 7 that allows users to quickly restore individual files that have been modified, damaged or even deleted.

It works by making automatic backups (every hour by default) of all files stored in the following folders: Contacts, Desktop, Favorites, and the Documents, Music, Pictures and Video Libraries. All other folders are ignored. However, if you want to include a folder other than the default ones, all you have to do is place it in a library.

By default, File History is turned off. Enable it as follows:

1 Connect an external drive to the PC. Typically, this will be a USB flash drive or external hard drive

2 Go to Control Panel, File History. Assuming you have correctly connected an external drive, you will see the following:

3 Click Turn on

All files in the above-mentioned folders will now be automatically backed up every hour. Note that existing backups are not over-written by new ones – each backup is kept so over a period of time, a file history is created. This enables a file to be restored from a backup created at a specific hour and day.

To restore a file, click "Restore personal files" from the link at the top-left of the window. Then browse to the required backup.

The only way to specify additional folders to be backed up is to add them to a library.

By default, backups are made every hour. However, this can be changed in Advanced settings.

Keep Windows Updated

Due to the ever-evolving threats posed by malicious software, it's essential to keep Windows updated. If it's not, its security measures, good as they are, will eventually be breached.

While Windows 8.1 is currently a very secure operating system, rest assured that even as you read this, many people are working on ways to circumvent its security features as they did (successfully) with Windows XP. To counter this, Microsoft releases a stream of updates, which plug security loopholes as and when they are discovered. While these can be downloaded manually by the user from the Microsoft website, this method has two inherent disadvantages:

● It can be a lengthy procedure so many people will quickly lose interest and simply not bother with it

● The user will forget to do it, or not do it frequently enough

A better way of keeping the PC updated is to use Windows Update. The option to set this up is offered during the installation procedure and if you didn't do so, we suggest you do it now:

1 Go to Control Panel, Windows Update. Then click "Let me choose my settings"

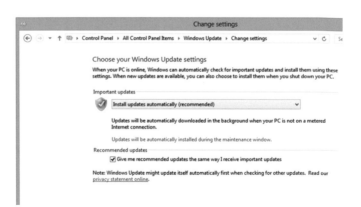

2 Select "Install updates automatically (recommended)"

Windows Update is a very good feature that works seamlessly in the background keeping the PC abreast of all the latest updates with no inconvenience to the user. Simply set it and forget it.

Hot tip

If you are concerned that Automatic Updates will slow your Internet connection, you needn't be. The utility uses unused Internet bandwidth to "trickle-feed" the updates download without affecting the user's browsing activities.

Hot tip

Windows Update is not restricted to just Windows. It will also update other Microsoft software on your PC.

Computer Quick Lock

Another way in which the security of your PC can be compromised is by a casual snooper. They may, actually, not be snooping at all – it could be a family member who sits down at the PC while you've popped out to the kitchen.

One way to prevent this is to log off. However, doing this will close all your running applications so you will have to restart them all when you log back on.

A much quicker way is to create a shortcut on the Desktop or Taskbar that will enable you to lock the PC instantly, should it ever be necessary to do so.

To do this:

1 Right-click the Desktop and select New, Shortcut. In the "location of item" box, type the following: rundll32.exe user32.dll,LockWorkStation

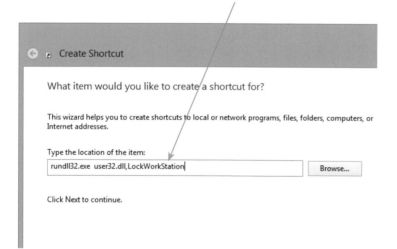

2 Click Next and give the shortcut a name, e.g. Lock PC

The shortcut icon will now appear on the Desktop from where it can be quickly accessed. Alternatively, you can drag it to the Taskbar.

If you don't like the look of the shortcut icon, you can change it to something more to your liking as described on page 92.

The account must be password-protected before it can be locked.

Be aware that there is a space between .exe and user. The text must be entered correctly for the shortcut to work.

117

Definitions are a list of known threats. As new malware programs are discovered on a daily basis, it's essential that Windows Defender is kept updated with the latest definitions in order to protect the PC.

Security on the Internet

The source of most dangers to PC owners is the Internet. Having learned from its mistakes with early versions of Internet Explorer, Microsoft has improved the security of recent versions. Here, we'll look at a couple of issues regarding Internet security and Windows 8.1.

The first concerns Windows 8.1's anti-malware utility, Windows Defender. If you open this in the Control Panel you'll see it's configured to do a quick scan. We suggest you change this to a full scan. Then check that the utility's spyware and virus definitions are up-to-date; if not, click the Update tab.

The second concerns the Enhanced Protected Mode feature. Briefly, in Enhanced Protected Mode, Internet Explorer 11 cannot modify user or system files and settings without user consent. Protected Mode requires the user to confirm any activity that tries to download something to the PC or start another program. By ensuring the user consents to these kinds of actions, the likelihood of automated and/or unwanted software installation is reduced. This feature also makes you aware of what a website is trying to do, thus giving you a chance to stop it.

However, while Enhanced Protected Mode is enabled by default in the app version of Internet Explorer, in the desktop version it is not. Thus users of the latter who are not "Internet savvy" or visit risky sites are advised to enable it as follows:

1 Go to Internet Options in the Control Panel and open the Advanced tab

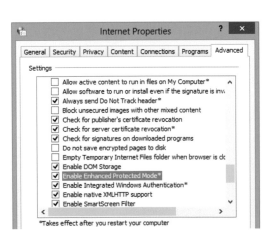

2 Click "Enable Enhanced Protected Mode"

Privacy Issues with Sync

A feature in Windows 8.1, and one that is sure to be popular with many users, is Sync. This enables settings and data to be synchronized across a number of Windows 8 devices.

For example, you may have a Windows 8.1 PC on which you keep your contacts and email account details. By using the same Microsoft account on your Windows 8.1 cell phone, this data will be automatically loaded on to your phone. Also, any subsequent changes to the data will be updated automatically, i.e. synchronized.

While this is undoubtedly convenient and will prove to be a real timesaver for many users, there are sure to be occasions when it is not desirable from a security point of view. For instance, if several people have access to one of your devices, you may not want your website passwords synced. Another scenario is your Personalization settings, which, by default, will be synced and applied to all of your Windows 8 devices – this is something you may not want.

The solution is to configure the Sync feature to disregard settings you'd rather not share across your devices. Do it as follows:

1 On the Charms bar, click Settings, Change PC settings, OneDrive. Then click Sync settings

2 As shown above, you will now see options for turning off synchronization for various features

Child Protection Utilities

The Internet is a minefield that can expose gullible and trusting kids to many different types of threat. All responsible parents will want to minimize, if not eliminate completely, the risks to which their children are exposed. There are many commercially-available programs available that help them to do this, such as Net Nanny, CyberPatrol, etc. The best of these applications enable parents to control and monitor every aspect of what the typical child might want to do on a computer and the Internet.

However, this book is about Windows 8.1 so we will look at what this operating system has to offer in the way of child protection. We'll start with Windows inbuilt utility - Family Safety. Go to Control Panel, Family Safety. In the dialog box that opens, you will be prompted to set up a user account for each child you want to protect.

By itself, the Family Safety utility does not offer much to get excited about. However, when used in conjunction with the Family Safety website (see next page), you can control pretty much anything your kids do, not only on the Internet but also on the PC itself.

Having created a new account, click its icon to open the settings dialog box. Here, you will be able to set parameters such as time limits, game ratings, and which programs can be run.

...cont'd

However, this application doesn't provide a monitoring facility. To do this, and more, click "Manage settings on the Family Safety website".

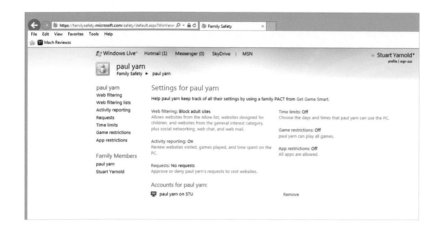

Don't forget

A big advantage of the Family Safety website is that you can monitor and control your children's Internet activities even when you are away from home.

This provides a web-based control panel (shown above) from which you can do the following:

- Block/allow specific websites

- Use web filtering to block unsuitable content. Different filters can be created for each child

- Block file downloads

- Control and monitor who your kids are communicating with via instant messaging software, such as Windows Messenger, and email

- Get monitoring reports on what your kids have been doing both on the Internet and the PC

- Access and adjust each child's safety settings from the Family Safety website, accessible from any PC

Used in conjunction, the Family Safety utility and Family Safety website not only enable parents to control everything their kids do on the Internet, they also provide a degree of protection to the PC by blocking potentially dangerous downloads, and access to programs and settings on the PC.

Risk-Free Internet Browsing

The Internet, as we all know, is the source of virtually all dangers faced by PC owners these days. No matter how tight your PC's security, no matter how careful you are, it is quite likely that something nasty will slip through the net.

So how is it possible to browse without any risk? The answer is to use a virtual PC when on the Internet. To build one, you need a virtual machine application such as Microsoft's Virtual PC, or Sun's VirtualBox; there are many others as well. These programs enable you to build a completely functional PC that runs within the program. Below, we see a virtual Windows 7 PC running in VirtualBox on a Windows 8.1 computer.

Hot tip

If you are running Windows 8.1 Pro or Windows 8.1 Enterprise, you already have virtual machine software. You need to install it first though:

Open Search and type "Turn Windows features on or off". Click the link, check the Hyper-V box and click OK. When the feature has been installed, you'll see a new Hyper-V Manager tile on the Start Screen. This will enable the creation of a virtual computer.

By default, a virtual PC is completely isolated from the host PC (the physical machine), thus anything that happens on it, such as a virus, or malware, does not affect the host in any way.

Furthermore, as you can install and run programs on a virtual PC, you can use it to evaluate downloaded software, safe in the knowledge that if the program is buggy, or otherwise suspect, it cannot mess up your physical computer.

In fact, any action at all that you may be wary of trying on your main machine, such as changing system settings, messing in the Registry, etc., for fear of causing problems, can be tried out perfectly safely on a virtual machine first.

If you are running Windows 8.1 Pro or Windows 8.1 Enterprise, you can use the Hyper-V virtual machine software built into Windows – see margin note. If not, use VirtualBox – a free download from **www.virtualbox.org/**

9 Installation/Setting Up

This chapter focuses on installation and setting up procedures. Among other things, you will learn the best way to install Windows 8.1, how to create a hard drive partition and calibrate a monitor.

Before carrying out a Windows reinstallation, make sure you have backed up any data you don't wish to lose. While it's rare, an installation can result in data loss.

Upgrading to Windows 8.1

When installing a new operating system, the option taken by most users is to simply install it over the top of the old one – a procedure known as upgrading.

The drawback with this method is that problems on the existing setup will be carried over to the new one. Typical examples of this are viruses and malware. There may also be third-party programs on the old setup that are corrupted and thus cause problems; these may also be carried over to the new setup. Furthermore, these issues can cause the installation of the new operating system to fail.

For these reasons, the best way of updating your operating system is to completely remove the old one first. Then, you install the new version. This method is known as a "clean install". However, there is a drawback – the procedure wipes the hard drive clean of all data, so you first have to make a backup of any data you don't want to lose and then reinstall all of your applications.

Because of this, you may prefer to go the upgrade route, in which case we suggest you first carry out the following steps. This will greatly improve the chances of doing it successfully:

1 Optimize your hard drive by running a disk defragmentation utility, such as Windows Disk Defragmenter

2 Run a disk checking utility, such Windows Chkdsk; hard drive errors are a common cause of installation problems

3 Check your system for viruses; these can stop an installation in its tracks. Having made sure your system is free of viruses, uninstall the antivirus program. Alternatively, you may be able to disable it in the BIOS. Antivirus software is well known for causing installation problems

4 Remove all programs from your Startup folder. Disconnect as much of your system's hardware as you can. Problems often occur during the hardware detection and configuration stages of an installation

Clean Installing Windows 8.1

There are two scenarios in which it may be necessary to do a clean installation of Windows. The first is when a new computer is being set up, and the second is when an existing installation is deleted and then replaced by a new copy because it is damaged in some way.

With Windows 8.1, the latter is no longer necessary, as a feature called Reset reverts a Windows installation to original factory settings. In the first scenario, however, a clean installation is still necessary and this is how you do it:

1 Start the PC and access the BIOS Setup program (see margin note). Open the Advanced BIOS Features page and scroll down to First Boot Device

```
          Phoenix - AwardBIOS CMOS Setup Ut.
               Advanced BIOS Features

   Virus Warning                [Disabled]
   CPU Internal Cache           [Enabled]
   External Cache               [Enabled]
   CPU L2 Cache ECC Checking     [Enabled]
   Quick Power On Self Test     [Enabled]
   First Boot Device            [CDROM ]
   Second Boot Device           [HDD-O]
   Third Boot Device            [CDROM]
   Boot Other Device            [Enabled]
   Swap Floppy Drive            [Disabled]
```

2 Make sure CDROM is selected. If not, use the Page Up/ Page Down keys to select it. Save any changes made and exit the BIOS

Having set the CD/DVD drive as the first boot device, place the Windows 8.1 installation disk in the CD/DVD drive and boot the PC. Shortly afterwards, you will see a message saying "Press any key to boot from CD…"

Do so, and Windows will begin loading its installation files to the hard drive.

3 At the first screen select your preferences – installation language, time and currency format, and keyboard method. At the next, click Install now

The key required to access the BIOS will be specified at the bottom of the first boot screen. It will also be in the motherboard manual. Usually it is either the Delete key or the F1 key.

125

All the tools required to do a clean install of Windows 8.1 are on its installation disk. So, you must set the CD/DVD drive as the first boot device.

...cont'd

4 Enter the product key to activate Windows and OK the license agreement. In the next screen select "Custom: Install Windows only (advanced)"

5 At the next screen, "Where do you want to install Windows?", select the required hard drive

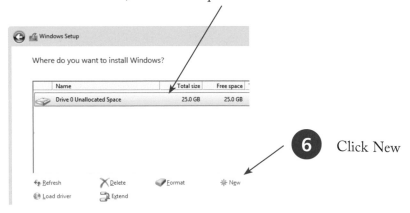

6 Click New

Hot tip

If you're not sure about setting the partition size in Step 7, just click Next. Windows will create a partition equal to the size of the hard drive.

7 Enter the required partition size and click Apply. Then click Next

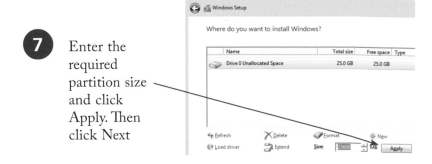

Follow the prompts to complete the installation.

Drive Management

Windows Drive Management utility enables users to manage their hard drives. They can create, format and resize partitions, create RAID configurations, and create and manage Mounted and Dynamic partitions.

Much of this will be well above the average user's head and is, in any case, beyond the scope of this book to adequately address. Therefore, we will restrict ourselves to a brief explanation of how to access the utility, how to create and format new partitions, and resize existing partitions. These are the applications that the typical user will be interested in:

1 Go to Control Panel, Administrative Tools. Then click Computer Management

2 When the Computer Management snap-in opens, click Disk Management

3 In the main window, you will see all of the hard drives installed in the PC (one in the example below), plus the CD/DVD drive

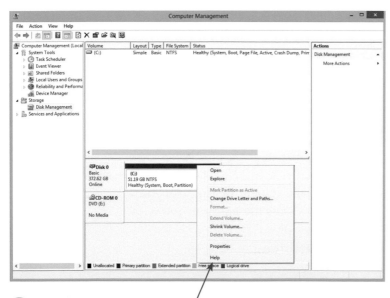

To avoid any confusion, note that the term "Volume", as used in the right-click menu shown on the left, is Microsoft parlance for a partition.

4 Right-click a drive to see the management options available to you

Hot tip

A partition is basically a container within a hard drive. Most PC manufacturers supply the PC with the hard drive partitioned to the maximum size, i.e. the full capacity of the drive. However, a partition can be split into any number of sub-partitions, each of which appears to Windows as a separate drive.

Hot tip

If you reduce the size of a partition, the amount by which it is reduced will become free space. Unless you use this free space to increase the size of a different partition or create a new one, it will be wasted.

...cont'd

Creating a Partition

In the example below, the PC has a single hard drive that has been partitioned to its maximum capacity. This means it has no free space. So before we can create a second partition on the drive, we have to first create some free space to allocate to it. This will be taken from the unused space on the existing partition.

1 Right-click the drive and click Shrink Volume

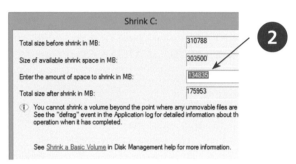

2 You will see the amount of space that can be freed. This is the maximum possible size of the new partition

3 Click Shrink. In the management window (below), you will now see the amount of space that has been freed

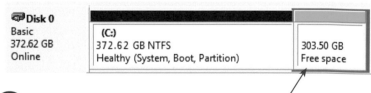

4 Right-click the area marked as Free space and select New Simple Volume; a wizard will now open. Click Next in each of the steps that follow and then click Finish. The new partition will be created and formatted with the NTFS file system. In This PC, you will now see a new drive – this is the partition you've just created

Resizing a Partition

To reduce the size of a partition, use the Shrink Volume command. To increase the size of one, first create some free space from a different partition, then use the Extend Volume command to add it to the desired partition.

Setting Up User Accounts

Windows allows the setting up of any number of user accounts, each of which can be individually configured in many ways (Desktop icons, wallpapers, screensavers, and so on).

This feature is particularly useful in a home environment where several family members all use the PC. By giving each their own account, which they can customize to suit their specific requirements and tastes; a single PC can be used without conflict.

It can also be useful in a single-user environment by enabling a user to create accounts for specific purposes. For example, one account can be set up for photo-editing with shortcuts to all the relevant programs placed on the Desktop. Another account can be set up as a home office, etc:

When two or more accounts are created, one of them must be an Administrator account. The person running this account will be able to set restrictions on what other account holders can and cannot do.

1 On the Charms bar, click Settings, Change PC settings, Accounts, Other accounts. Then click Add a user

2 You will now have options of signing in with an existing Microsoft account or creating a new one. You can also create a local account by opting to sign in without a Microsoft account, plus create a child account

The disadvantage of a local account is that the user won't be able to download apps from the Microsoft store, and also that they won't be able to synchronize their settings and data across different devices and computers.

A useful application of user accounts is to password-protect the main account and then create standard accounts for the kids. They can use the PC but won't be able to compromise its security or performance due to the limitations placed on standard accounts.

The advantage of an expandable space is simplified storage management.

Don't forget

You can mix and match drives of any type and size when creating a Storage Space.

Create a Virtual Drive

Of critical importance in the increasingly digital world we all inhabit is how to keep that digital data safe. Related factors include how and where to store the data and the cost of doing so.

We saw on page 33 how a technology known as RAID can be used to provide data protection. RAID is available in either software or hardware versions and, of the two, hardware is by far the most reliable as it is completely independent of the operating system. The problem with hardware RAID is that it requires a separate RAID controller card and good ones are not cheap.

A feature in Windows 8.1 provides a much more cost-effective method of data protection although, being a software solution, it is still not as robust as hardware RAID. The feature is known as Storage Spaces and can be accessed in the Control Panel.

Storage Spaces provides three very useful benefits: an easily-expandable space in which to store data, RAID data protection, and low cost.

Expandable Space

A Storage Space is essentially a virtual drive comprised of a number of physical drives. The drives can be of any type, e.g. SATA, USB, SAS, etc., and of any size. The capacities of the drives are combined to produce a Storage Space. The capacity of the Storage Space can be increased at any time by simply adding another drive – this is its main advantage; a single drive of unlimited capacity can be created quickly and easily.

The capacity of a Storage Space is set by the user and it is not restricted to the total capacity of the physical drives. For example, a 100GB storage space can be created from 10GB of physical drive space. This is achieved with a technique known as thin provisioning, which gives the appearance of more space than actually exists. As more data is added to the storage space, or virtual disk, the size of the real file grows as necessary.

When the capacity of storage space has used up, it can be reset to a larger size.

Data Protection

When a Storage Space is created, the user has the option to add data protection of the same type used in RAID.

...cont'd

Three types of fault tolerance are offered: Simple (striping), Mirroring and Parity. For example, with 2-way mirroring, two copies of a space's data are stored on separate drives. Thus if one drive fails, the data is recoverable from the other.

Cost

Storage Spaces offers nothing that cannot be found elsewhere – there are quite a few other companies offering similar products. However, without exception, these cost hundreds of dollars, require specific hardware, and provide expansion options that are limited in scope.

Storage Spaces, on the other hand, costs nothing, requires no hardware other than the drives, provides a virtual drive of unlimited size, and is very simple and quick to set up. The procedure is:

1 Go to Control Panel, Storage Spaces. The opening dialog box will show you all the drives on your system that are compatible with Storage Spaces, as shown below

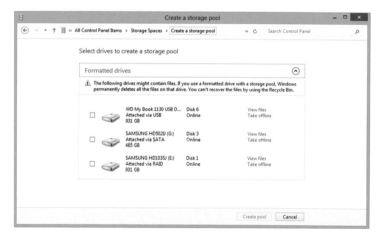

2 Select the drives you want to use for the Storage Space and click Create pool

3 In the new window, you will see options for the drive letter to use, the type of resiliency (simple, two-way mirror, etc), and the size of the pool. When you have made your choices, click Create Storage Space

Hot tip

One caveat with Storage Spaces is that they are not bootable, i.e. you cannot install an operating system on one.

Keep your Files & Settings

One of these days you're going to decide that you need a new computer. Having bought it, you will then need to redo all of the customization and configuration settings, such as Internet/email settings, display settings, Taskbar configuration, and so on. You will also have to transfer all your files, such as music and video, to the new PC. It will be a time-consuming procedure.

A USB flash drive is an ideal way to use the Easy Transfer utility.

Windows 8.1 provides two features that will help enormously. The first is the OneDrive app. By default, all your personalization and app settings, plus other stuff such as Internet favorites and History, passwords, and many Windows settings are automatically saved to your OneDrive storage. All you have to do is configure the new PC with the same Microsoft account used on the old PC, and all the settings will be seamlessly transfered to it.

With regard to transferring your data, this is easy with the Windows Easy Transfer utility. To access it, type "easy transfer" in the Charms bar search box. Click "Windows Easy Transfer" and a wizard will open as shown below:

The first step will be the Easy Transfer utility copying itself to a writable medium, such as a CD/DVD disc or flash drive. You then run it on the old PC where it will guide you through the steps necessary to save your old files and settings to the medium.

Then go back to the new PC, connect the medium and run the utility again. Your data files will be transferred across and stored in exactly the same locations.

Another good way is to use an Easy Transfer cable (this has a USB plug on either end). It is also possible to use a network.

You can transfer the following with Windows Easy Transfer:

- User Accounts
- Documents
- Music
- Email
- Pictures
- Videos

Run Older Programs on Windows 8.1

When you install programs on your Windows 8.1 PC, you may come across one or two that refuse to run: this will be due to incompatibility issues.

Before you throw them away, try installing them with the Compatibility Mode wizard. This will recreate the Windows environment for which they were designed and will, in most cases, get them running.

Go to Control Panel and click Action Center. At the bottom-left, click Windows Program Compatibility Troubleshooter. Click Next and after a few moments you will see a dialog box showing you a list of all the programs on the PC. Select the one you're having trouble with and click Next.

Another way of applying compatibility settings is to right-click the program's executable (setup) file. Click Properties and then open the Compatibility tab. From here, you can choose an operating system that the program is known to work with.

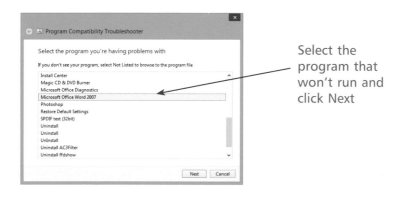

Select the program that won't run and click Next

If a program won't install at all, the method described here won't work. In this case, do it as described above.

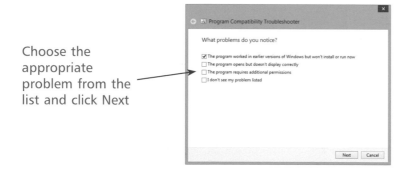

Choose the appropriate problem from the list and click Next

Once a program has been set up successfully, it will use the compatibility settings every time it is run.

Windows will try to fix the issue. If the problem hasn't been resolved, click "No, try again with different settings" to repeat the procedure with other possible causes.

Calibrate your Monitor

Have you ever noticed when printing an image that the print-out looks somewhat different to the image on the PC? For example: it's brighter or darker, the colors aren't the same, or it looks washed-out?

It could be that the printer settings are not correct but it's far more likely that your monitor is incorrectly calibrated. Windows 8.1 includes a monitor calibration utility, and you can access it by going to Control Panel, Display. At the top-left of the Display dialog box, click "Calibrate color":

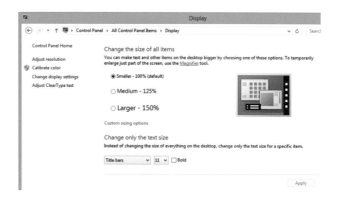

You will then be taken through a series of dialog boxes that will enable you to adjust your monitor's gamma, brightness, contrast, and color balance settings.

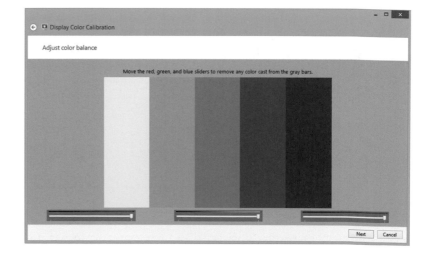

Hot tip

Before calibrating your monitor, do the following:

Allow the monitor to warm up for at least 30 minutes so that it's at its full operating temperature. This will ensure a consistent display.

Set your desktop background to a neutral gray. Bright colors and patterns surrounding an image make it difficult to accurately perceive color.

Install Windows 8.1 Quickly

Here we show to install Windows from a USB flash drive. The advantages of installing Windows in this way are threefold:

- Speed – Windows will install much quicker

- You will have a much more robust copy of the installation disk (which you can now put in a drawer and forget about)

- You can install Windows on PCs with no DVD drive

The procedure is as follows:

1 Plug the USB flash drive into the PC. Open This PC (press Win + X and click File Explorer) and make a note of its drive letter

2 On the Start screen, open a command prompt by typing command. Right-click on Command Prompt and select Run as administrator

3 Type the following entries at the command prompt pressing Enter after each one

diskpart
list disk

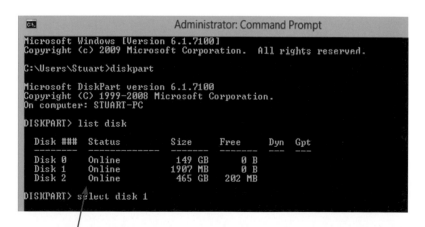

```
                    Administrator: Command Prompt
Microsoft Windows [Version 6.1.7100]
Copyright (c) 2009 Microsoft Corporation.  All rights reserved.

C:\Users\Stuart>diskpart

Microsoft DiskPart version 6.1.7100
Copyright (C) 1999-2008 Microsoft Corporation.
On computer: STUART-PC

DISKPART> list disk

  Disk ###  Status         Size     Free     Dyn  Gpt
  --------  -------------  -------  -------   ---  ---
  Disk 0    Online          149 GB     0 B
  Disk 1    Online         1907 MB     0 B
  Disk 2    Online          465 GB   202 MB

DISKPART> select disk 1
```

You will see a list of all the drives installed on the PC. Determine which entry relates to the USB drive (see bottom margin note). Usually it will be Disk 1.

Hot tip

The USB drive must have a capacity of no less than 4GB.

135

Hot tip

If you are not sure which is the USB drive, go to This PC, right-click the USB drive and click Properties. Under Capacity, you will see the size of the USB drive. Go back to the command prompt window and the drive of corresponding size is the one you want.

...cont'd

4 Now, format the USB drive by entering the following commands, pressing Enter after each one:

select disk x (x is the USB drive number, e.g. 1)
clean
create partition primary
select partition 1
active
format fs=ntfs
assign
exit

You'll now have a formatted USB flash drive ready to be made bootable. This is done by using the Bootsect utility that is supplied with the Windows 8.1 installation disk. To do this:

1 Insert your Windows disk into the CD/DVD drive and then change to the installation disk's boot directory where the Bootsect utility is located. Do this by going back to the command prompt window and typing the following, pressing Enter after each entry:

d:
cd d:\boot (d is the drive letter of your CD/DVD drive)

2 Still at the command prompt, type:

bootsect /nt60 x: (x is the drive letter of the USB drive).

Press Enter and close the command prompt window

3 Now, copy the entire contents of the Windows 8.1 installation disk to the USB drive

Your USB boot drive is now ready to go.

Before you use it, don't forget that you must first change the boot order in the BIOS so that the system will boot from the USB drive. This is done in the same way as setting the CD/DVD drive as the boot drive – see page 125.

Don't forget

For this tip to work, the flash drive must be made bootable.

Don't forget

When using your flash drive to install Windows, you must first set the BIOS boot order so that the USB is the first boot device.

10 Shortcuts

Virtually every action that can be done with a mouse can also be done with the keyboard. This chapter shows how, and also explains some other useful shortcuts.

Switch Applications Quickly

Windows supplies two handy tools designed to help users differentiate between running applications and quickly switch between them.

Windows Flip

To use the Flip feature, hold down Alt and press Tab. This opens a panel in the middle of the desktop that shows a thumbnail of each running application. Each time you press Tab, a different application is selected and its name appears at the top of the panel. When you release the Alt key, the panel disappears and the last application selected becomes the open window on the display.

Hot tip

If you have recently bought a new keyboard, you may find it has a Flip key. Many keyboard manufacturers provide this.

You can also select applications with the arrow keys and the mouse.

Taskbar Thumbnails

Resting the pointer over a Taskbar item displays a live thumbnail of the window that shows its content. The thumbnail is displayed whether the window is minimized or not.

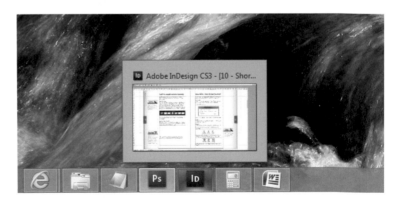

Moving the pointer over the thumbnail shows a full-screen preview of the window – click the thumbnail to switch to the application. It is also possible to close applications, and play/pause video and music from the thumbnail previews.

One-Click Shutdown/Restart

Users who like to do things quickly will appreciate the following method of instantly shutting down, restarting or logging off.

Shutdown

Create a desktop shortcut (right-click, New, Shortcut) and enter the text shown below in the box:

SHUTDOWN -s -t 01

Click Next and name the shortcut Shut Down. Then click Finish.

Restart

As above but this time type SHUTDOWN -r -t 01 in the box. Name the shortcut Restart.

Log Off

As above, but this time type LOGOFF in the box. Name it Log Off.

When you have finished, you will see the following icons on the Desktop.

Using the tip detailed on page 92, you can change the icons to something more interesting or representative, as shown below.

Finally, drag the icons to the Taskbar where they can be accessed instantly.

You can also create hotkey shortcuts for your new Shut Down, Restart and Log Off commands – see page 140.

Hotkey Shortcuts

There will be occasions when you want to open a program but don't wish to close the current window so that you can get to it. For example, you may be doing a tax return online and need to open the calculator.

A hotkey shortcut is the answer:

1 Right-click the program and select Properties

2 The Properties dialog box will open

3 Click in the Shortcut key box (this will be reading None)

140

Calculator Properties

General | Shortcut | Security | Details

Calculator

Target type: Application
Target location: system32
Target: %windir%\system32\calc.exe

Start in:
Shortcut key: Ctrl + Alt + C
Run: Normal window
Comment: Performs basic arithmetic tasks with an on-screen

Open File Location | Change Icon... | Advanced...

OK | Cancel | Apply

4 Now press the key you want to use as the shortcut key (C in the example on the left)

5 The Shortcut key box will now read Ctrl + Alt + C

6 Click OK, and from now on you can open the application by pressing Ctrl + Alt + C

Windows Key Shortcuts

Most standard keyboards have one, or even two, Windows keys. These are situated near the space bar and have a logo of a flying window printed on them. The key is commonly known as the Win key.

Windows keys

Keyboard shortcuts can also be found within applications. Alongside most menu commands, you will see shortcut key combinations.

With either of these keys you can quickly open a number of applications on your computer.

The table below shows which keys can be used in conjunction with the Windows key and what they do:

Keys	Action
Win + D	Minimize or restore all windows
Win + SHIFT + M	Undo minimize all windows
Win + E	Open Computer
Win + F	Open Windows Search utility
Win + R	Open Run dialog box
Win + Enter	Launch the narrator
Win + BREAK	Open System Properties dialog box
Win + L	Lock Computer
Win + T	Cycle through Taskbar programs
Win + U	Open Ease of Access Center

On page 146, we see some more Win key shortcuts that can be used with the Windows 8.1 interface.

Easy Email

This is a handy tip for those of you who do a lot of emailing. Instead of starting your email program each time you want to send a message to someone and then clicking the Create Mail button on the menu bar, you can achieve the same thing from the Desktop with one click. Here's how to do it:

1 Right-click the Desktop and select New, Shortcut. You will see the following dialog box

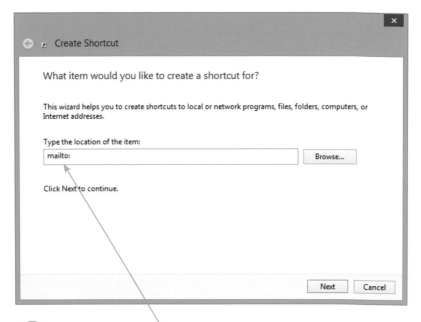

2 In the box, type: mailto: Then click Next and give the shortcut a suitable name

You will now see a new email icon on the desktop. Click it and an open email message window will appear.

Taking this a step further, you can have the message window open with the address already filled in. Do this by entering the email address immediately after mailto:

For example, if you enter "mailto:stuart.yarnold@ntlworld.com" your email will open with this address in the To: box, as shown below. Then, type in your message and click Send.

Taskbar Searching

A little used feature in Windows is the Address toolbar. This lets you do a number of things directly from the Desktop:

1 Right-click the Taskbar and select Toolbars, Address. You will now see an address box on the Taskbar next to the notification area

The first thing you can use the Address toolbar for is to launch websites; you don't need to open Internet Explorer first. Just type in the address and press Enter, or click the arrow.

Furthermore, once you've launched a site in this way, you can subsequently relaunch it by clicking the down arrow at the side of the box and selecting the site from the History list.

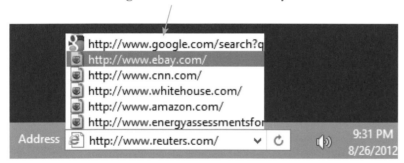

You can also conduct an Internet search from the Address toolbar. To do this, just enter your search keyword and press Enter on the keyboard:

Microsoft's Bing default search engine will open with the results of the search.

Finally, you can launch programs from the Address toolbar if you know their executable name. For example, typing "winword" will open Microsoft Word.

Keyboard Shortcuts

In certain situations, using the keyboard can be a much easier way of controlling a computer. The following is a selection of useful keyboard shortcuts:

The following are some useful shortcuts that work with most applications:

- CTRL + O – opens a document from within a program

- CTRL + N – opens a new document

- CTRL + S – saves work in progress

General Shortcuts	
CTRL + C	Copy the selected item
CTRL + X	Cut the selected item
CTRL + V	Paste the selected item
CTRL + Z	Undo the last action
DELETE	Delete the selected item
SHIFT + DELETE	Delete an item permanently
F2	Rename the selected item
CTRL + RIGHT ARROW	Move to the beginning of the next word
CTRL + LEFT ARROW	Move to the beginning of the previous word
CTRL + DOWN ARROW	Move to the beginning of the next paragraph
CTRL + UP ARROW	Move to the beginning of the previous paragraph
CTRL + SHIFT + ARROW	Select a block of text
CTRL + A	Select all items in a document or window
F3	Search for a file or folder
ALT + ENTER	Display properties for the selected item
ALT + F4	Close the active item or exit the active program
ALT + SPACEBAR	Open the shortcut menu for the active window
CTRL + F4	Close the active document
ALT + TAB	Switch between open items
CTRL + ALT + TAB	Use the arrow keys to switch between open items
ALT + ESC	Cycle through items in the order they were opened
F6	Cycle through screen elements in a window
F4	Display the address bar list in Windows Explorer
SHIFT + F10	Display the shortcut menu for the selected item
CTRL + ESC	Open the Start menu
F10	Activate the menu bar in the active program
RIGHT ARROW	Open the menu to the right, or open a sub-menu
LEFT ARROW	Open the menu to the left, or close a sub-menu
F5	Refresh the active window
ALT + UP ARROW	View the folder one level up in Windows Explorer
ESC	Cancel the current task
CTRL + SHIFT + ESC	Open the Task Manager
SHIFT when inserting a CD	Prevent the CD from automatically playing

Internet Explorer Shortcuts	
F1	Display Help
F11	Toggle between full-screen and normal views
TAB	Move forward through items
SHIFT + TAB	Move backwards through items
ALT + HOME	Go to your home page
ALT + RIGHT ARROW	Go to the next page
BACKSPACE	Go to the previous page
SHIFT + F10	Display a shortcut menu for a link
UP ARROW	Move toward the beginning of a document
DOWN ARROW	Move toward the end of a document
HOME	Move to the beginning of a document
END	Move to the end of a document
CTRL + F	Find on this page
F5	Refresh the current web page
ESC	Stop downloading a page
CTRL + O	Open a new website or page
CTRL + N	Open a new window
CTRL + W	Close the current window (if you have only one tab open)
CTRL + P	Print the current page or active frame
ENTER	Activate a selected link
CTRL + I	Open Favorites
CTRL + H	Open History
CTRL + J	View Downloads
ALT + T	Open the Tools menu
Working With Tabs	
CTRL + CLICK	Open links in a new tab in the foreground
CTRL + SHIFT + CLICK	Open links in a new tab in the background
CTRL + T	Open a new tab in the foreground
CTRL + TAB	Switch between tabs
CTRL + W	Close current tab
ALT + ENTER	Open a new tab in the foreground from the address bar
CTRL + 9	Switch to the last tab
CTRL + ALT + F4	Close other tabs
Using the Address Bar	
ALT + D	Select the text in the address bar
F4	Display a list of addresses you've typed
CTRL + ENTER	Add "www." and ".com"

Hot tip

Many Internet Explorer operations are actually quicker using the keyboard. For example, the Backspace key is much easier to use than the Back button. Also, try using the Up and Down arrow keys to scroll through pages. The Home and End keys are other useful keys that take you quickly to the beginning and end of pages.

Hot tip

The list on this page contains just some of the keyboard shortcuts available for Internet Explorer. You can find many more by going to http://windowshelp. microsoft.com/Windows (type keyboard shortcuts in the search box).

...cont'd

New Windows 8 Interface Shortcuts	
Win + B	Switch to the (classic) Windows Desktop
Win + C	Open the Charms Bar
Win + D	Show the Desktop
Win + E	Open Computer
Win + F	Open the Search panel
Win + H	Open the Share charm
Win + I	Open the Settings charm
Win + K	Open the Connect charm
Win + L	Lock the computer
Win + M	Minimize the selected Explorer window
Win + O	Lock the screen rotation
Win + P	Switch Displays
Win + Q	Search (within) apps using the search panel
Win + V	Cycle through notifications
Win + W	Open the Settings search panel
Win + X	Open the Power User menu
Win + Z	Open the app bar
Win + Shift + V	Reverse cycle through notifications
Win + Page Up	Move tiles to the left
Win + Page Down	Move tiles to the right
Win + Shift + .	Move the Snap split to the left
Win + .	Move the Snap split to the right
Win + Spacebar	Switch input language and keyboard layout
Win + Tab	Cycle through apps
Win	Toggle Windows 8 Start Screen and last run app

The most useful of these keyboard shortcuts are the ones that open the various Windows menus, such as Win + C (Charms bar), and the Win key by itself, which toggles between the Start Screen and the most recently-run app.

Hot tip

Type the main part of an address and then press CTRL + ENTER. This will automatically add the www. and .com to complete the address. This only works for addresses ending with .com, however.

11 The Internet

The Internet is a wonderful resource for information, entertainment, software and business. This chapter details a wide range of tips that include extending the basic functionality of Internet Explorer 10, useful features of this new browser, and how to improve the efficiency with which you use the Internet.

No More Broken Downloads

Anyone who downloads data from the Internet will, at one time or another, experience the irritation of an unexpected disruption to their download.

Unfortunately, Internet Explorer doesn't have the ability to automatically resume interrupted downloads, so you then have initiate the process again. Furthermore, it may be necessary to start the download from the beginning. This is not too bad if it is a small download, but if you are downloading a large file you could have wasted a lot of time.

The solution is to use what's known as a "download manager". Programs of this type monitor a download and if it is interrupted for whatever reason, will resume it from the point at which the download stopped; thus, you don't have to start again from the beginning.

They also offer other useful features, such as automatic scheduling, automatic redial (for dial-up modem connections) and details regarding file size, download time, and so on.

One of the most popular download managers is GetRight (shown below). This is available at **www.getright.com**

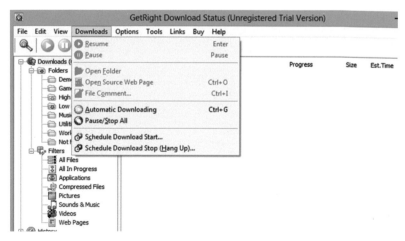

A good download manager can also increase download speeds considerably. If the file is held on several servers (which is quite common), the program will switch between the servers automatically selecting the one that offers the best, i.e. fastest, download conditions.

Cut Down on the Scrolling

Have you ever opened one of those web pages that seems to go on forever? To find something specific, you have to keep scrolling down the page and, if you miss it, then scroll back up.

Let's say you are researching an article on Abraham Lincoln. Your search leads you to one of these long pages, the content of which is the American Civil War. All you want is information about Abraham Lincoln and his role in it, though; nothing else. So instead of endless scrolling down the page to find references to him, try the following:

1   On the keyboard, press Ctrl + F

Just below the address box, you will now see a "Find" toolbar.

2   Type Abraham Lincoln into the search box

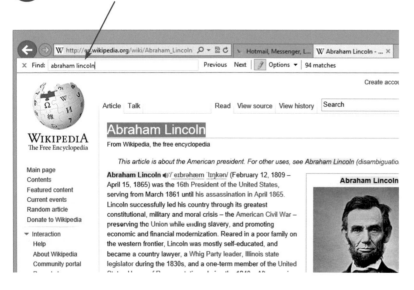

149

At the end of the Find toolbar, you will see the total number of instances of the keyword on the page.

Internet Explorer will automatically scroll down to the first instance of the word, or phrase, entered. It will be highlighted in yellow so you can't miss it.

3   To find the next instance, press Enter, and so on

Disable SmartScreen

SmartScreen is a feature that has been around for a while now in Internet Explorer and has three main functions:

Phishing is a scam that works by setting up a fake website identical to that of a respected institution, such as a bank (well, maybe not a bank but you get the point). Victims are sent an email with a link to the fake website asking them to log on. When they do, their username and password are stolen. The consequences of this are obvious.

150

- As the user browses the Internet, it analyzes the web pages for signs of anything suspicious

- It checks all sites visited against a dynamic and continuously updated list of known phishing sites

- It checks all files downloaded from the Internet against a list of known malicious malware

Windows 8.1, however, takes SmartScreen a step further by integrating it in the operating system itself. As a result, in addition to the above, it will automatically block attempts to run any program that it doesn't recognize.

Windows protected your PC

Windows SmartScreen prevented an unrecognized app from starting. Running this app might put your PC at risk.

Publisher: Unknown Publisher
App: ResophNotes.msi

Run anyway Don't run

While the blocking can be over-ridden, many users are going to find the need to do so irritating and unnecessary. For those who don't need it, SmartScreen can be disabled:

1 Go to Control Panel and open Action Center. On the left, you'll see a "Change Windows SmartScreen settings" link. Click this to open the following dialog box:

Users for whom privacy is an issue should be aware that SmartScreen automatically sends data to Microsoft about every application the user installs.

Windows SmartScreen

What do you want to do with unrecognized apps?

Windows SmartScreen can help keep your PC safer by warning you before running unrecognized apps and files downloaded from the Internet.

◉ Get administrator approval before running an unrecognized app from the Internet (recommended)

○ Warn before running an unrecognized app, but don't require administrator approval

○ Don't do anything (turn off Windows SmartScreen)

OK Cancel

Some info is sent to Microsoft about files and apps you run on this PC.
Privacy statement

2 Disable SmartScreen

Keep Up with the News

Many websites, such as news agencies, offer a service called RSS Feeds. This service automatically feeds information, such as news headlines, sports scores, etc., at regular intervals to interested subscribers.

Internet Explorer has a built-in RSS reader that enables users to subscribe to, and read, any number of RSS feeds without having to visit the websites providing them.

To use this feature, you first have to find an RSS service and then subscribe to it:

Feeds work best with a broadband connection.

1 When you visit a website that provides a feed, the Feed button will turn Orange. Click the button to see what the feed offers, then click the feed itself

CNN.com - Top Stories
You are viewing a feed that contains frequently updated content. When you subscribe to a feed, it is added to the Common Feed List. Updated information is automatically downloaded to your computer and can be viewed in Internet Explorer and other programs. Learn more about feeds.

Add this feed to iGoogle

You can also configure Internet Explorer to play an alerting sound when you open a web page that contains a feed. Go to Internet Options in the Control Panel and click the Content tab. Then click Settings under Feeds.

151

2 A new window will open showing all the articles available in the feed. At the top of the window, you will see a Subscribe to this feed link, as shown above

3 Click the link to add the feed to Internet Explorer's Favorites Center and to the Common Feed List for sharing with other programs

To see a list of the feeds you have subscribed to, open the Favorites Center and click Feeds.

To view one, click it and Internet Explorer will open the page.

Hot tip

To get the best out of file-sharing, you really need a broadband connection, as many of the files available for download can be several gigabytes in size.

Beware

File-sharing networks are awash with viruses and malware. Not only that, but the file-sharing programs themselves may add malware to your system. Don't get involved in this activity if you want to keep your PC as clean as possible.

File-Sharing

File-sharing is a very popular Internet activity. It makes use of specialized peer-to-peer networks and software, which allow users to connect directly to the computers of other users in the same network. The purpose of it all lies in the name – file-sharing. Each user can designate specific files on their PC which they are willing to share.

To take part in this activity, you need a file-sharing program. These are available as a free download on the Internet and there are dozens of them (go to **www.download.com** and enter file-sharing in the search box).

Simply download and install the program, designate which files you want to share with other users, and you're all set to go. Good examples of this type of application are Emule (**www.emule-project.net**) and BitLord (**www.bitlord.com**).

Of all the file-sharing programs, Emule (shown below) is considered to be the best. It is also free of all adware and spyware, something that cannot be said for many of them.

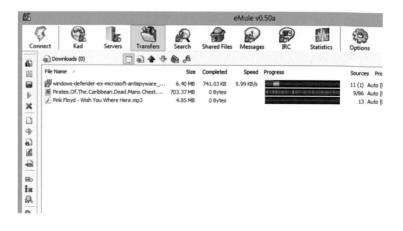

When using these programs, there are two things to be aware of: first, some of them may install malware on your PC; be wary of this.

Second, while the use of the program is legal, the downloading of copyrighted material is not; you do this at your own risk.

Get More Search Providers

A useful feature in Internet Explorer is the ability to search directly from the address bar – there's no need to go to a search engine. Not surprisingly, though, results from a search are taken from Microsoft's search engine, Bing.

Should you wish to use a different search engine, you can set this up as described below:

1 At the top-right of the Internet Explorer window, click the Tools icon

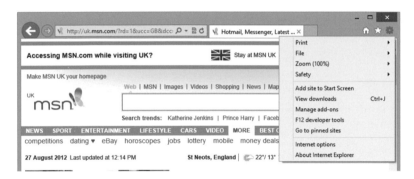

Hot tip

When you add a new search provider to Internet Explorer, you are given the option to make it the default provider. If you do, all searches made from the search box will be conducted with this provider.

153

2 Click "Manage add-ons" and then in the Window that opens click Search Providers. In the same Window, at the bottom, click the "Find more search providers..." link

3 You will now be presented with two pages of search providers from which to choose

Hot tip

If you want to set your new search provider as the default provider, click its entry in the "Manage Addons" window and click "Set as default".

Quick Internet Searching

Type the word "tiger" in Google and you will get millions of pages to look through. These will range from the Tiger Lily restaurant in Shanghai, Tiger Woods the golfer to, not surprisingly, pages about tigers. Finding something specific may take a long time.

To help users narrow their searches, all the major search engines offer an Advanced Search. This will offer various options, such as language-specific searches, and searches restricted to pages updated within a specific time frame, etc.

However, before you try these, the following simple search aids may be all you need.

The + Operator

Most search engines exclude common words such as "and" and "to", and certain single digits and letters. If you want to make sure a common word is included in the search, type + before it.

For example:

world war +1 (make sure there is a space between the + and the previous word).

The - Operator

The - operator allows you to exclude words from a search. For example, if you are looking for windows (glass ones), type:

windows -microsoft

This will eliminate millions of pages devoted to the various Windows operating systems.

The OR Operator

The OR operator allows you to search for pages that contain word A OR word B OR word C, etc. For example, to do a search on camping trips in either Yosemite or Yellowstone national parks, you would type the following:

"camping trips" yosemite OR yellowstone

Phrase Searches

By enclosing your keywords in quotation marks, you will do a phrase search. This will return pages with all the keywords in the order entered.

For example, "atlanta falcons" will return pages mainly concerning the Atlanta NFL team. Most pages regarding Atlanta (the city) or Falcons (the birds) will be excluded.

Combinations of Operators

To further narrow your searches, you can use combinations of search operators and phrase searches. Using our atlanta falcons example, typing "atlanta falcons" -olympic games -birds of prey -city, will remove several million pages of search results.

Numrange Searches

Numrange searches can be used to ensure that search results contain numbers within a specified range. You can conduct a numrange search by specifying two numbers, separated by two periods with no spaces.

For example, you would search for computers in the $600 to $900 price bracket by typing: computers $600..900

Numrange can be used for all types of units (monetary, weight, measurement, and so on).

You may, at some stage, come across the phrase "Boolean Operators" with regard to search engines. These are derived from Boolean Logic, which is a system for establishing relationships between terms. The three main Boolean operators are:

- OR
- AND (equivalent to +)
- NOT (equivalent to -)

The most useful operators are: - (NOT), and quotation marks (phrase searching). These two operators can whittle search results that would otherwise be several million, down to a few hundred pages.

Repair Internet Explorer

Internet Explorer is a highly complex piece of software and (as with Windows itself) it can, over time, become corrupted to the extent that it no longer works properly or little niggles and errors creep in.

Typically, you will begin seeing error messages such as "Internet Explorer has encountered a problem and needs to close". When Windows itself malfunctions, it can be repaired by reinstalling it. However, there is no way to do this with Internet Explorer.

However, there is a way to repair it:

 Open Internet Options in the Control Panel and click the Advanced tab

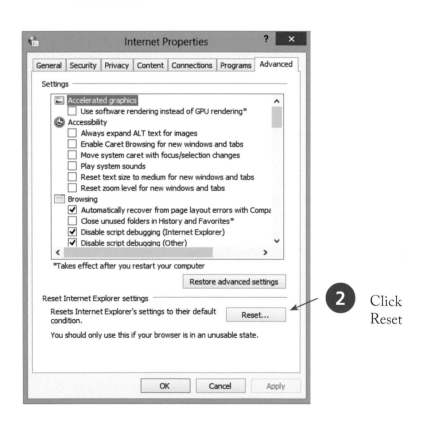

This deletes all add-ins and customizations, and gets you going with a fresh version of Internet Explorer.

Hot tip

If Internet Explorer stops responding repeatedly, try the following:

- Scan the computer for malware
- Clear the contents of the Temporary Internet Files folder

Hot tip

Resetting Internet Explorer removes all changes that have been made to its settings from the time of its installation. It does not delete your Favorites and Feeds though.

Get to Grips with Tabs

Browser tabs are another useful feature in Internet Explorer. Using them is straightforward enough so, rather than describing the obvious, we'll show you some neat tricks that you may not have noticed yet.

Multiple Home Pages

Rather than having Internet Explorer open with one default page, tabs allow you to have as many as you want. Open the Internet Options utility in the Control Panel and in the Home Page box on the General tab, type in the addresses of the websites (when you've typed one, press Enter and then type the next one, and so on).

The next time you open Internet Explorer, it will automatically open all the websites, each in a separate tabbed window.

Categorized Groups of Tabs

Let's say you like to dabble in stocks and shares. You use the Internet for your share dealings and probably have several related websites in your list of Favorites. Rather than opening each website individually as you would have done previously, tabs allow you to open them all simultaneously.

To do it, open all the websites in separate tabs and click "Add to Favorites". Then click "Add Tab Group to Favorites". In the next dialog box, enter a name for the group, e.g. Stocks. Then click Add.

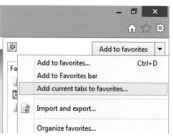

Hot tip

To close a specific tab when you have several open, you have to click the tab in order to reveal the X button. A quicker way is to click anywhere in the tab with the mouse's scroll wheel.

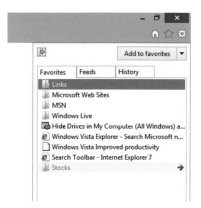

The next time you want to see how your shares are doing, click the Favorites button and then click the arrow alongside your Stocks folder. All the websites in the group will now open in separate tabbed windows.

Alternatively, click the folder itself to show a list of all the websites.

157

Back Up your Favorites

A large, well-organized list of Favorites takes a long time to build up and is literally impossible to replace. Losing it can be nothing short of a calamity.

If you have such a list and don't relish the prospect of having to build it up again, back it up as follows:

1 From Internet Explorer's File menu, click Import and Export; this opens the Import/Export wizard. Click Next and you will be presented with three options

2 Select "Export to a file"

3 Select the Favorites folder to backup everything

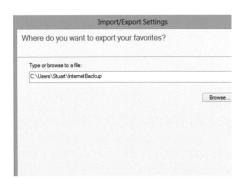

4 Browse to your backup location. Click Next and then Finish

Flip Ahead Browsing

Internet Explorer 11 offers a browsing feature called Flip Ahead, which is designed to make browsing multi-page articles, or search results, easier.

It works by placing a forward and back button on either side of the browser window in an easily-accessible position. The buttons are only visible when the mouse is moved to either side of the window – this prevents the feature being intrusive.

Flip Ahead is only active in web pages that contain a link to "go ahead" to another page. The image below shows how the buttons look:

Flip backwards   Flip forwards

By default, Flip Ahead is disabled. To enable it in classic Internet Explorer, go to Control Panel, Internet Options. Click the Advanced tab, scroll down to "Enable flip ahead with page prediction" and check the box.

To enable it from the Start screen, open a browser window and then open the Charms bar by pressing Win + C. Click Settings, Privacy and scroll down to Flip ahead and enable it.

Note that whichever version of Internet Explorer you enable Flip Ahead in, it will also be enabled in the other version.

Web Slices

A Web Slice is similar to an RSS feed. Basically, it lets you subscribe to a specific section of a web page and then alerts you when the content of the slice has changed; for example, the current temperature, or an auction price.

When you visit a web page that offers slices, you will see a green icon on the Command bar:

A list of websites that provide web slices can be found at www.ieaddons.com

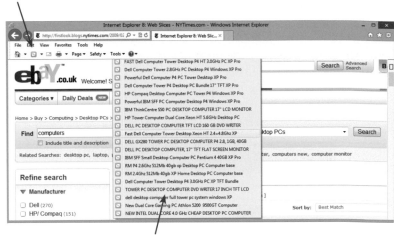

Click the arrow to the side of the icon to reveal the available slices

To subscribe to a slice, just click it. It will be added as a link on the Favorites bar, as shown below:

When the Web Slice is updated, the link on the Favorites bar will appear with bold formatting. You can then click the link to see the updated content.

To delete a slice when you've finished with it, right-click it on the Favorites bar and click Delete.

Speed Up Internet Explorer

There are many browser add-ons that extend the versatility and capability of Internet Explorer. Typical add-ons include toolbars, download managers, Adobe Reader, etc.

The downside of these add-ons is that they all take time to load, and thus prevent Internet Explorer from starting as fast (and often running) as it otherwise might. They can also be the cause of other problems, such as pop-up advertisements, browser lock-ups, and even a reduction in the performance of the PC.

If you are experiencing problems with your browsing, or just want Internet Explorer to run as fast as possible, disabling any add-ons you may have is a good place to start:

Another thing you can do in the Manage Add-ons window is check how long it takes for each add-on to load. This information is available in the Load Time column. If you see one that is taking an abnormal length of time to load in comparison to the others, try disabling just this one.

1 Go to the menu bar and click Tools, Manage Add-ons. You will see a list of all the add-ons installed on Internet Explorer, as shown below

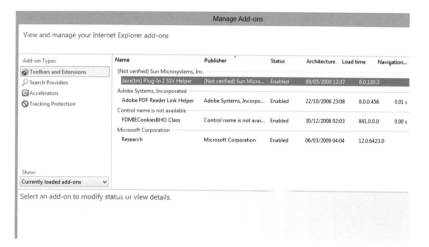

2 Select each add-on in turn and click the Disable button. This enables you to run Internet Explorer without any, or just some, add-ons

Running it without any add-ons enabled should give Internet Explorer a definite boost in speed.

Accelerate your Browsing

Finding what you want on the Internet can be a long-winded procedure that often involves moving from one site to another. For example, you may be on holiday and want to identify and then locate a good restaurant.

First you have to decide which restaurant you are going to use by doing a search engine search. Having established this, you then use a different site, e.g. Google Maps, to find out how to get to it.

Internet Explorer's Accelerator feature allows you to do both without leaving the first site. Using our restaurant example, you have picked one called The Four Seasons. Highlight the name and you will see a blue accelerator icon appear to the side of it:

Click the icon and you will see a list of accelerators installed in Internet Explorer. Select "Map with Bing" and a map of the restaurant's location will be generated and displayed:

Clicking the map will open a full web page in a new tab that includes additional information from the mapping service.

This is just one example of how accelerators can be used.

Hot tip

A list of accelerators can be found at www.ieaddons.com

Easy Text Selection

When selecting text in a web page it can be difficult to select precisely what you want without also selecting adjacent text, and objects such as images and tables, as shown below:

Internet Explorer's Caret Browsing feature has been introduced to solve this problem. This enables you to use the keyboard instead of the mouse to make selections, and it offers much more precise control.

To activate Caret Browsing, press F7. Then place the cursor at the beginning of the text block you want to select, press and hold down the Shift key and highlight the text with the arrow keys.

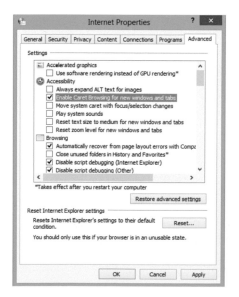

Some users may find this feature so useful that they might want to have Caret Browsing permanently enabled. This is very easy to do.

On Internet Explorer's menu bar, click Tools, Internet Options. Then click the Advanced tab and check "Enable Caret Browsing..."

163

Miscellaneous Tips

Quick Printing
Rather than printing out an entire page when all you want is a few lines or a paragraph, do the following:

1 Select the required text, right-click and select Print

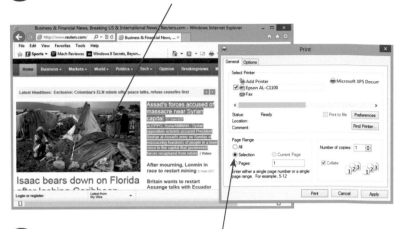

2 In the printer's software, select Selection. Only the selected text will be printed

Print Scaling
When you print a web page, Internet Explorer automatically scales it to fit within the margins of your paper. Should you prefer to do this yourself, however, do the following:

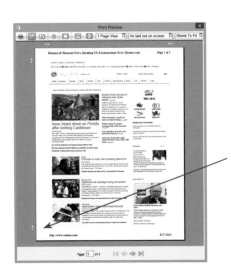

1 Click the arrow next to the Print button and click "Print Preview"

2 In the Print Preview window, grab the resize handles and drag them to resize the page

Get in Close

Internet Explorer allows users to zoom in on a page. This is useful for those whose sight is not so good or where text is hard to read:

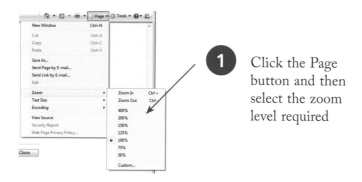

Click the Page button and then select the zoom level required

Hot tip

If you don't see a Page button, right-click at the top of a Internet Explorer window and select Command bar.

2 Another way is to click the Zoom button at the bottom-right of the page. Note that you must first enable the Status bar from Toolbars on the View tab

Hot tip

You can also control the Zoom function with the keyboard:

- CTRL + PLUS SIGN = zoom in by 10%

- CTRL + MINUS SIGN = zoom out by 10%

- CTRL + 0 = zoom to 100%

Stop the Kids Downloading

Have you ever worried about what your children are downloading while you're not around? This tip will put your fears to rest:

1 Go to Internet Options in the Control Panel. Click the Security tab, click the Custom Level button and then scroll down to the Downloads section

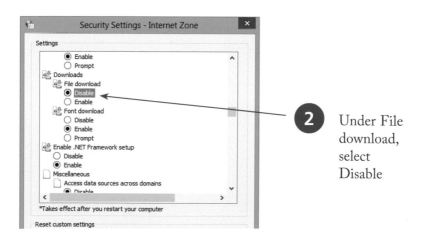

2 Under File download, select Disable

Hot tip

The Family Safety utility provides another way of preventing your kids downloading from the Internet.

165

Hot tip

Another, more laborious, way is to simply download the entire page using the File, Save As, command.

...cont'd

Override Disabled Right-Click Menus

Have you ever visited a website that has the right-click menu disabled, thus preventing you from copying or downloading? Well, in case you ever come across another of these websites, you'll be pleased to know there is a solution.

All you have to do is use the context menu key on your keyboard. This is located between the right-hand Windows logo key and Ctrl key. Just press it to bring up the right-click menu.

An alternative method is to press the Shift key in conjunction with the F10 key.

Image Resizing

Internet Explorer has a feature called Automatic Image Resizing, the purpose of which is to resize a picture if it is too large to fully display in the browser window.

If you don't want this, there are two ways to deal with it:

● Position the pointer over the image and it will turn into a mini magnifying glass. Simply click the image to restore it to its full size

● Disable the feature. Do this by going to Internet Options in the Control Panel. Click the Advanced tab and scroll to the Multimedia section. Here, you will find the disable option

Hot tip

Internet Explorer's Favorites bar is a very useful feature that enables you to create, and quickly access, shortcuts to your favorite websites. To open it, click the Views tab, Toolbars, Favorites bar. To add a webpage shortcut to it, right-click on the page, select Add to favorites, Favorites Bar.

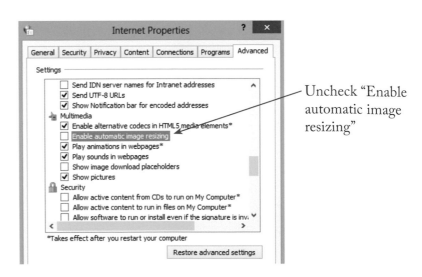

Uncheck "Enable automatic image resizing"

12 Email

In this chapter, we look at probably the most popular PC application of all – email. Learn how to safeguard your messages and account settings, how to access your email from anywhere in the world, avoid spam and viruses, plus much more.

Setting Up an Email Account

Unlike its predecessor, Windows 7, Windows 8.1 provides users with an email program. However, this is in the form of an app that is only available from the Start screen.

As with all Windows 8.1 apps, the email app is very basic and provides the user with few options. That said, it works and is very easy to set up. Users who want more control over their email will need to look elsewhere, though – see page 169.

see page 169

The Windows 8.1 Email App

To set up an email account in Windows 8.1, click the Mail app. If you didn't set up a Microsoft account when installing Windows, you'll be asked to do so now as shown below:

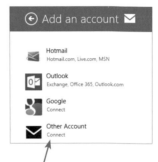

Having done so, you will then see the Add an account screen where you choose the type of account. (Note that if you already have a Microsoft account, you'll be taken directly to this screen.)

The final step is to enter your email address and password in the Add your account dialog box as shown below:

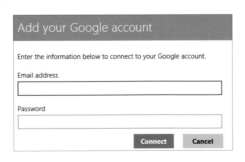

Click Connect and the account will be set up with no further input from the user. However, if you are using an "Other" type of account, some settings may need to be entered manually.

Further accounts can be added by opening the Mail app and then selecting Settings from the Charms bar. Then click Accounts and Add Account.

Access what few configuration settings are available with the email app by opening the app. Then from the Charms bar, select Settings, Accounts, Check Settings.

If you try to set up a POP account, you'll see a message stating that POP accounts cannot be used with the email app. However, we managed to do it by entering POP instead of IMAP in the IMAP box.

Windows Live Mail

As already stated, Windows 8.1's email app provides few configuration options for the more advanced email user. If this is you, you will need to install a third-party program.

Mozilla, author of the FireFox web browser, provides the free Thunderbird email client, while another free email program with a very good reputation is Eudora. Both of these are good choices and can be downloaded from the manufacturers' websites. If you do an Internet search, you will also find a multitude of other email programs. This might be a good time to try out a few and see how you get on with them.

Alternatively, you can opt to stay with Microsoft. Its current free offering is Windows Live Mail, an updated version of the Windows Mail program that was provided with Windows Vista.

If you are migrating from Vista and used Windows Mail, you will probably decide to go with Windows Live Mail. This can be downloaded from the Windows Live Essentials website at **www.download.live.com**

Setting up an account in Windows Live Mail couldn't be simpler; all you need to do is enter your email address and ISP password and then click Next. The account will be created almost instantly:

The menu bar in Windows Live Mail is disabled by default. Get it back by clicking the menu icon at the top-right and then clicking "Show menu bar".

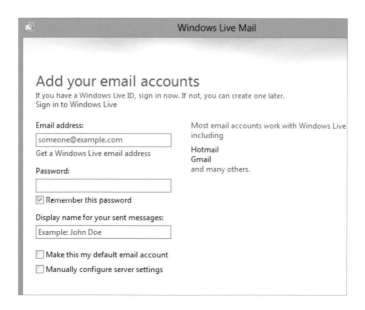

Back Up your Emails

The provision of email facilities is a very important function of the modern-day computer, and just as people often like to keep personal letters, they also like to keep their emails. It is also an important means of business communication and these messages usually need to be kept as records.

Windows Live Mail provides an easy way to back up your messages and contacts:

1 From Windows Live Mail's File menu, select Export email, Email messages

170

2 Select Microsoft Windows Live Mail

3 Browse to your backup folder and click Next

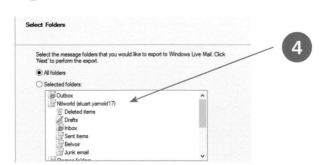

4 Select the email folders to back up, click Next and the backup will be created

---

Hot tip

It's always a good idea to store backups on a separate medium. In the case of email account settings, which are very small files, a USB flash drive is ideal.

Back Up your Email Account

Backing up your email account is perhaps not as important as backing up your email messages because the account can be set up again if necessary. Nevertheless, it can be a nuisance, particularly if you have several accounts, as many people do.

Windows Live Mail makes it easy:

1 From the File menu, click Export Email, Account

2 Select the account to be backed up and click Export

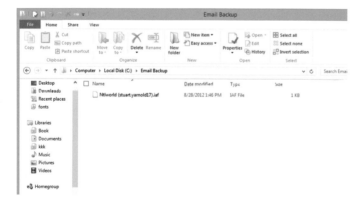

3 Browse to the backup folder and click Save

Should you ever need to reinstall the account, or accounts, simply reverse the above procedure, only this time click Import in Step 2.

If you just want to back up a particular message, double-click it and select Save As from the File menu. You can then save it where you like.

Should you ever lose your emails, you can restore them from the backup by selecting Import, Messages from the File menu.

Users of Microsoft Outlook can download an automatic backup utility at **www.microsoft. com/downloads** Enter "personal folders backup" in the search box and click Go.

Open Blocked Attachments

Viruses transmitted by email are almost always contained in an attachment to the email. However, the attachment must be opened by the user before the virus can be released.

To prevent this, Windows Live Mail has a virus protection feature that prevents any attachment that it considers unsafe from being opened. When this happens, you will see a red bar at the top of the email saying the file has been deactivated. An example of this is shown below:

Hot tip

Windows Live Mail can be configured to read email in plain text format. When you enable this setting, no dangerous content in the email is run. Do it as follows:

- From the File menu, click Options, Mail

- Click the Read tab and then check the "Read all messages in plain text" check box

172

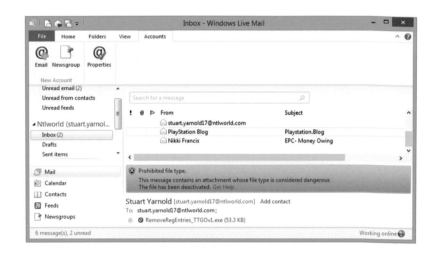

This is all very well and the feature will prevent people opening dangerous attachments, either through ignorance or carelessness. However, if you think an attachment is safe – you recognize the sender, for example – you need to know how to open it.

Also, if you share your email address only with people you trust, as many people do, you may want to disable the virus protection feature completely.

To do this:

1 From Windows Live Mail's File menu, click Options, Safety Options

2 Click the Security tab

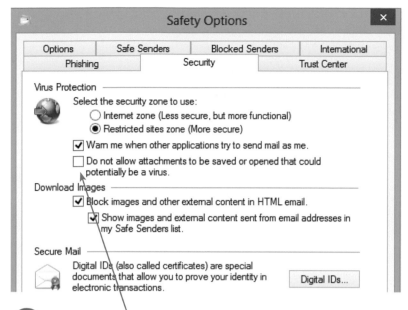

3 Uncheck the "Do not allow attachments to be saved or opened that could potentially be a virus" check box under Virus Protection and then click OK. Now you will be able to open the attachment

Be careful when opening attachments. This is the most common way for viruses to be transmitted. Before you open any attachment, take a look at its file extension and if it is of a dangerous type just delete it.

If you really want to read the message though, open it in plain text format – see the margin tip on page 172.

173

Of course, if you do decide to disable this protection feature, you run the risk of inadvertently opening a dangerous attachment. Therefore, you need to be able to recognize when one has arrived in your Inbox because Windows Live Mail is not going to warn you. To do this, look at the extension of the file in the attachment. This will be below the red warning bar, as shown below:

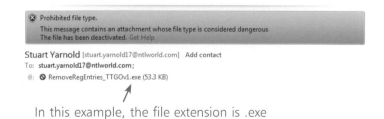

In this example, the file extension is .exe

Now refer to the tables on pages 174-175. These will show you which file extensions are safe to open and which are not. Once you are confident the file is OK, you can open the attachment.

High-Risk File Attachments

An email attachment ending in any of the file extensions in the table below can, potentially, be carrying a virus.

Beware

Note that in general, image formats are considered to be safe. The exception to this is the JPEG format, which can carry a virus.

File Extension	Description
.ADE	Microsoft Access Project extension
.ADP	Microsoft Access Project
.BAS	Visual Basic Class module
.BAT	Batch file
.CHM	Compiled HTML help file
.CMD	Windows NT Command Script
.COM	MS-DOS application
.CPL	Control Panel extension
.CRT	Security certificate
.EXE	Application
.HLP	Windows help file
.HTA	HTML application
.INF	Setup information file
.INS	Internet communication settings
.ISP	Internet communication settings
.JS	JScript file
.JSE	JScript Encoded Script file
.LNK	Shortcut
.MDB	Microsoft Access application
.MDE	Microsoft Access MDE database
.MSC	Microsoft Common Console document
.MSI	Windows installer package
.MSP	Windows installer patch
.MST	Visual Test Source file
.PCD	Photo CD image
.PIF	Shortcut to MS-DOS program
.REG	Registry file
.SCR	Screensaver
.SCT	Windows Script Component
.URL	Internet shortcut
.VB	VBScript file
.VBE	VBScript Encoded Script file
.VBS	VBScript Script file
.ZIP	Zipped folder

Low-Risk File Attachments

The file types in this table are extremely unlikely to be carrying a virus and can be considered to be safe.

File Extension	Description
.GIF	Picture – Graphics Interchange Format
.TIF or TIFF	Picture – Tagged Image File Format
.MPEG	Movie – Motion Picture Expert Group
.AVI	Movie – Audio Video Interleaved
.MP3	Sound – MPEG compressed audio
.WAV	Sound – Audio
.TXT or TEXT	Notepad document
.BMP	Picture – Windows Bitmap
.ICO	Picture – Icon
.PNG	Picture – Portable Network Graphic
.WMF	Picture – Windows Meta File
.LOG	Log file

In an effort to disguise the extension of the file in which the virus is hidden, some virus writers give the file two extensions. The dangerous one is always the last. If you ever get such an attachment, delete it immediately.

Open Blocked Images

Another security feature in Windows Live Mail prevents images included in web pages from being opened automatically. When this happens, the areas in the email message that contain images display a red X placeholder rather than the image itself.

There are two reasons for this:

● It protects the user from potentially offensive material

● It helps prevent spam. Many spammers include an image URL in their emails. This notifies the spammer when the message is opened, thus confirming that the address is real

Should the user wish to see the image, they just have to right-click and click Download Images. It is also possible to disable the feature so that all images are shown automatically when the message is opened.

Do this by clicking Options on the File menu and clicking Safety Options. Then click the Security tab and uncheck "Block images and other external content in HTML email".

An attachment extension to be particularly wary of is .zip. This catches many people out as most PC users are familiar with the Zip compression format and see no threat in it.

Global Email Access

Email has become a very important facet of our lives and, for many, it is essential – to the point of having to be able to access it at any time wherever in the world they may be.

The simplest way to have global access to your email is to use a web mail service, such as those provided by Google (Gmail) and Microsoft (Hotmail). With these services, both sending and receiving email is done online rather than from a program on the PC. Furthermore, all messages are stored on the provider's server, which means they can be accessed from any PC, anywhere in the world.

The problem with web mail comes when an Internet connection is not available at the time you need to access your saved messages. Because they are online, you won't be able to do so.

The solution comes in the form of an option found in nearly all email programs. This enables the user to send and receive email from their computer and, at the same time, save copies of those emails on their ISP's server.

As a result, their email messages will be accessible both on their PC and online. Furthermore, should they lose, or accidently delete, a message, they'll have a backup from which to restore it.

As Windows Live Mail is be used by many people, we'll show you how to do it with this program:

1 From Windows Live Mail's File menu, click Options, Email Accounts

Don't forget

Another issue with web mail is the fact that many of the providers subject users to a bombardment of advertisements in return for a free account. Indeed, many of them are known to trawl through users' messages so as to better target these ads.

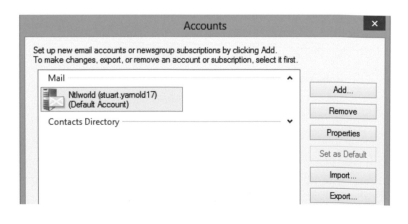

2 Select your email account and click Properties

3 Click the Advanced tab and then check "Leave a copy of messages on server". Click Apply and you're done

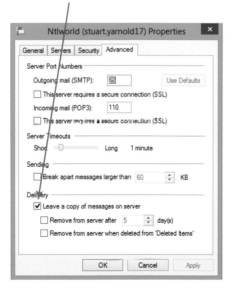

You'll now be able to manage your email from your PC, and also have access to it on your ISP's server from any computer.

A Spam-Free Inbox

Spam accounts for approximately three-quarters of email traffic worldwide. That adds up to several billion emails every day.

If you find yourself the recipient of an endless stream of advertisements, too-good-to-be-true offers, etc., what can you do about it?

The first step is to close your account and then set up a new one – this will stop it immediately. You then need to make sure the new account is kept out of the spammers' reach. Observing the following rules will help:

- Make your address as long as possible. Among other things, spammers use automated generators that churn out millions of combinations (aaa@aol.com, aab@aol.com, and so on). It won't take them long to catch up with bob@aol.com.

- Never post your address on a website. Spammers use spiders that trawl the Web looking for the @ symbol, which is in all email addresses.

- If you need to give an address to access a web page, give a false one. Alternatively, set up a specific account with filters that direct all received emails to the deleted items folder. Use this account when an address is asked for.

- Never click the "Unsubscribe from this mailing list" link in a received spam email. This tells the spammer that your address is real and could open the floodgates.

- Make use of your email program's filters (Message Rules in Windows Live Mail). Properly configured, these can cut out a lot of spam.

- Use a Bayesian filter. This is available as a third-party product and integrates with your email program. Its effectiveness is due to the fact that it is "intelligent" and thus, can be trained in much in the same way as Voice Recognition software.

  The Bayesian filter examines all aspects of a message, as opposed to simple keyword checking that classifies a message as spam on the basis of a single word or phrase. Once set up and trained, a Bayesian filter will eliminate 99% of spam.

Organize your Emails

If you're like most people, your Inbox will be bulging at the seams with messages from weeks, months and even years ago. This tip shows how to tidy it up and then keep it tidy:

1 Create a new message folder for each of your contacts

2 Go through the Inbox and move your messages to the new categorized folders. Delete any you don't want

Having created order out of chaos, you need to make sure it stays that way, and without having to do it manually. To this end, you now need to set up your email program's message filters to do the job automatically:

3 From Windows Live Mail's menu bar, click the Folders tab and then Message rules

A big advantage of organizing your emails in this way is when you need to locate an old message for rereading. Instead of having to search through an over-flowing Inbox, you will know exactly where it is.

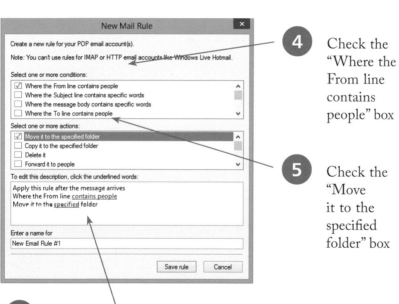

4 Check the "Where the From line contains people" box

5 Check the "Move it to the specified folder" box

6 Click "contains people" and in the dialog box that opens, enter a contact's email address. Then click "specified" and click the folder you created for the contact. Repeat the above procedure for all of your contacts

From this point on, all messages from the contacts you have specified will be moved automatically to the designated folders.

Automatic Picture Resizing

As anybody who regularly uses email will know, email programs allow users to either insert images directly into the email or attach them as a file.

The problem with this is that unless the image has been reduced in size in an imaging program (a process of which many people are unsure), it is possible to end up sending a huge picture file that will take the recipient ages to download. Most people find this extremely irritating, as it can occupy their connection for a considerable length of time. This is particularly so if they use a dial-up connection.

Windows saves the day with its Email Picture Resizing utility:

1 Right-click the image you want to send with your email, select Send To and then Mail Recipient

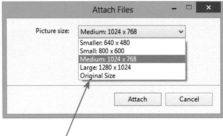

2 Select the required option, e.g. Small, Medium, Original Size, etc., and then click Attach

3 Click OK and an email message window will open with the resized image attached. All you have to do is type in the address and the text before sending the message

A couple of things to be aware of are:

● Pictures resized in this way are converted to the JPEG format, which you may or may not want

● Some image formats (Photoshop's PSD, for example), cannot be converted by the utility, and thus cannot be resized – they will be attached to the email but at the original size

Don't forget

You can resize any number of pictures at the same time – you are not restricted to just one.

Hot tip

Be wary of using the Small and Smaller resize options. While these reduce the size of files enormously, they also reduce the quality of the images considerably.

13 Multimedia

Multimedia has always been one of the most popular uses of PCs. Here, we look at various ways of enhancing your multimedia experience, and show you some recommended software.

Most of the codec packs are designed for specific versions of Windows. If you do decide to install one, be sure it is compatible with the Windows version you are using.

Play any Media File

Video and audio files in their raw state are huge in size. To make it easier to manage these files, e.g. downloading, copying, etc., compression techniques are used to reduce their size.

The type of program that does the compressing is known as a codec and there are hundreds of them. Two well-known examples are DIVX for video and MP3 for audio.

However, once a file has been compressed, it must then be decompressed before it can be played. The decompression is done by the same codec that compressed the file originally.

This gives rise to a long-standing problem for computer users; they have a media file but are unable to play it because the required codec is not installed on the PC.

There are a couple of ways to resolve this issue. One is to check the file with a program that will analyze it and tell you which codec is required to play it. One such program is GSpot – see page 201 for more details.

The second way is to download and install a codec pack, which contains codecs for virtually all the many types of media file. Note that while Windows 8.1 provides the most commonly-used codecs, there are still many that it does not.

There are quite a few of these codec packs available on the Internet and if you decide to go down this route, we suggest you do a bit of research before actually installing one. Some of them can cause more problems than they solve.

One codec pack that the author has evaluated and found to be good is the Windows 8 codecs pack. You can download it from **http://shark007.net/ win8codecs.html**

This application does just what it says on the can; it installs all the codecs you are ever likely to need, without also installing any superfluous features, such as bundled media players, etc.

Build a Home Entertainment Center

One of the reasons that Home Entertainment Centers (HECs) have become so popular is that they combine all the devices necessary to keep the average family entertained into a single unit. Not only does this save space, they only need one power point and there are no complex connection issues. Another is that all the various functions can be operated with a single remote control.

Unfortunately, these systems are not cheap. So, rather than shelling out mega-bucks for an off-the-shelf solution, consider building one around the PC instead.

Requirements

The modern computer provides most of the hardware needed to build a basic HEC. You've got a monitor to watch TV and video, a DVD player to play discs, and speakers to listen to music. The only other things you'll need are a TV tuner, maybe a Blu-ray player, and software to integrate and control the devices.

Many owners of Windows 7 PCs already have the software in the form of Windows Media Center (WMC) and so, for an outlay of about $100 (*correct at time of printing*) for a decent TV tuner with a remote control, will be ready to go. All they have to do is install the TV tuner and then run WMC's setup wizard. Users of Windows 8.1 will have to buy a copy of Windows Media Center.

Considerations

The problem with the basic setup described above is that PCs are inherently unsuitable for use in a living room, which is where the HEC will be used. PCs are noisy and usually nothing much to look at. If you can live with these limitations though, there's nothing holding you back. Move the PC into the living room and, with the aid of the remote control, you'll be able to watch/record TV, play your music and videos, look at your photos, and even browse the Internet (if your monitor or TV is large enough) without ever leaving your armchair.

However, for the reasons mentioned above, you may not wish to have the PC in the living room. Alternatively, you may want to build a more sophisticated system that can be used in more than one room. In either case, you will have to incorporate your HEC devices into a network.

The beauty of an HEC is that everything can be operated with a single remote control.

Blu-ray players are available for PCs.

Windows Media Center is available as an add-on for users of Windows 8/8.1.

...cont'd

An extender connects a device to a network, enables it to access the media content of the PC, and allows it to be remotely controlled.

Hot tip

A simple way of creating a wired network is to use HomePlug. This system uses the electrical wiring in the house to form the network.

Networked HECs

In a networked HEC, each device (TV, Hi-Fi system, etc.) is connected to the PC via a Media Extender (see margin note). The connections are made in one of two ways:

- **Network cable** – this is known as a wired network and uses network cables (available from any good PC store) with Ethernet plugs at each end. These plug into Ethernet sockets on both the PC and the extenders.

- **Radio link** – this is known as a wireless network as the devices are connected by a radio frequency. In this setup, the PC has a wireless network adapter, and the extenders are wireless versions to which the devices are connected by an Ethernet cable. The network is set up using the Windows Network wizard (available from the Network and Sharing Center in the Control Panel).

Of the two types, a wired network is the best option in terms of performance and reliability. It does, however, require cables to be run to wherever a networked device is to be located. Wireless networks are much easier to set up as there is no cabling involved, and are also much more versatile as the devices can be moved to wherever they are required on an as-and-when basis.

Connections

Whichever option you go for, it will be necessary to make some physical connections, e.g. TV to PC, TV to extender, etc. For a high-quality picture, an HDMI connection is recommended. This will be found on most modern video cards, extenders, and most LCD TVs. A DVI connection will also be acceptable. HD Component Video works well but is not commonly found on PCs. All of these connections can support high-definition TV.

Applications

By connecting your HEC devices to a network via an extender, you can use them in any location. The extender's remote control will enable you to access any type of media on the PC, wherever it is situated.

You can also incorporate other types of device in the network to extend its range of uses. For example, it is quite simple to set up a home surveillance system by adding cameras to the network.

Keep the Discs in the Drawer

One of the most irritating things about playing games on a computer is the constant need to insert and change discs. This can also be the eventual cause of physical damage to the discs.

While most game manufacturers allow their games to be run directly from the hard drive, thus eliminating the need to use the discs, there are still some that don't. Some people try to get round this by copying the disc to the hard drive and then installing the game from there. Unfortunately, this rarely works – when you try to run the game you usually get a "No disk in CD drive" error message. This is manufacturers' copy protection at work.

The solution to the problem is a virtual drive. This is an emulated drive created and controlled by software. The user creates an image of the game's disc on the hard drive, which can be played in the virtual drive; the real disc is not required at all.

There are many of these applications available on the Internet. A good one is Virtual CD, available at **www.virtualcd-online.com** You can either buy the full version or try out a trial version:

Hot tip

Virtual drives can be used with any type of program; they are not restricted to games. Although most applications now offer an "install to disk" option, there are still many that do not. A virtual drive is the answer.

Installed games   Virtual drives

Hot tip

Most CD/DVD-authoring programs also provide a virtual CD drive. With these though, you will only have one drive.

Virtual drive programs can create up to 23 virtual drives, which means you can have up to 23 different games pre-loaded and ready to go. You can put the discs in a drawer and forget about them. Also, as the games are being played from the hard drive, they will perform better.

Another advantage of these programs is that they can override most manufacturers' copy protection methods.

Graphic Formats Unraveled

When using graphics files in documents, presentations, web pages, or for printing, it is important that you choose a format that is suitable for the task in hand. Using the wrong one can result in poor-quality images, images that take an eternity to open, or images with unnecessarily high file sizes.

The first thing to realize is that image formats are split into two main groups: Vector and Raster.

Vector

Vector images are composed of mathematically-defined geometric shapes, e.g. lines, squares, circles, etc., and are typically generated by drawing applications such as Adobe Illustrator and Microsoft Visio. Two notable advantages of this format are:

Many of the vector formats (including the three mentioned on the right), can also handle raster data. These are often called Metafiles.

- Image size can be increased to an almost unlimited degree without noticeable loss of image quality.

- Individual parts of an image can be edited. For example, if a particular image contains both text and objects, it is possible to change the text's formatting (font, color, size, etc.).

Vector formats tend to be proprietary, i.e. specific to a particular program. However, many drawing applications allow you to save an image in formats used by other popular vector programs.

Commonly-used vector formats include:

- **WMF** – this is the standard vector file used in Microsoft products, such as Microsoft Office

- **PCT** – this is the standard vector format used by Macintosh operating systems

- **EPS** – this format can be used on a variety of platforms, including Macintosh and Windows

Raster

In raster files, the image is comprised of a grid, or matrix, of tiny squares called pixels. This allows extremely complex pictures to be recorded, typically photographs, and it's this characteristic that makes them the most widely-used format.

The main drawback is that in their raw state, they can be very large files. However, this is compensated for by the fact that this format can be heavily compressed to reduce file size.

With regard to compression, there are two types, lossy and lossless:

- **Lossy** – with this method, unnecessary data is permanently stripped out of the file, thus reducing its size. Although it may be imperceptible, the quality of the image is reduced.

- **Lossless** – here, data is temporarily removed from the file. When the file is opened, the data is replaced. Thus, there is no loss of image quality.

Commonly-used raster formats are:

- **JPEG** – a lossy format, JPEG's main advantage is the fact that it can be highly compressed. This makes it ideal for use in web pages, and where a low file size is required. It can also handle 24-bit color, and so can be used for professional printing (although there are better formats for this).

- **GIF** – this is a low-size lossless image format, which is mostly found on websites where it is used for small low-quality images, such as advertising banners, clip art, etc. Use this format if you want the lowest possible file size and the quality of the image is not important.

- **PNG** – this is an advanced version of the GIF format and it offers several advantages, such as better color support and compression. PNGs are lossless.

- **TIFF** – this is a lossless format offering features that make it the ideal format for professional printing. File sizes are high but image quality is excellent.

Summary

For web pages where quality is not important, or low file size is, use GIF or PNG. Otherwise, use JPEG.

For general computer use, e.g. storing and viewing your holiday snaps, JPEG is the recommended format.

For professional printing of photographs, use the TIFF format.

There are several variants of the JPEG format. These include: JP2000, JPM, and JP3D. These are designed for more specific uses, such as volumetric imaging (JP3D), and usually require a plug-in.

If an image contains both drawing objects (vector) and photographs (raster), use a metafile format such as EPS.

Editing your Photos

Calibrate the Monitor

The first thing you must do is calibrate the monitor. If it is incorrectly set up, no matter how carefully you edit your images, when you print them, or view them on a different monitor, they will look different. You may even make them worse.

Calibration software should be bundled with your monitor. If not, use the calibration utility provided by Windows – see page 134.

Convert the Image to a Lossless Format

As we saw on page 187, image formats are either lossy or lossless. Every time a lossy image is edited, some loss of image data occurs. Thus, the more times it is edited, the worse the end result. Lossless images, on the other hand, can be edited any number of times with no loss of quality.

So, before you edit any image of the lossy type, convert it to a TIFF, which is lossless. Having edited the image, convert it back to the original file type. It only takes a few seconds and ensures that the original image quality is retained.

Brightness and Contrast Adjustments

All image editors provide brightness and contrast controls. Many also have an auto one-click setting that does the job automatically. While both can work well, often the result is less than optimal.

A better, and more reliable, way is to use the image editor's Histogram control. This presents a graphical representation of the image showing its color distribution in terms of brightness and darkness. The left of the graph represents black and the right represents white.

Consider the following example of a badly under-exposed picture:

If you have an image that cannot be replaced, make a copy and use that for editing. If you mess it up, you've still got the original.

Before you edit a photo, convert it to a TIFF file first. This can be done with the editing program. Then reopen it to start editing.

The imaging program provided by Windows is Windows Photo Viewer. Unfortunately, it doesn't provide any editing features. If you're serious about your photos, we suggest you acquire a more capable imaging program.

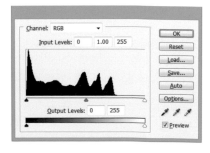

The image's Histogram shows that its data is over to the left of the graph, i.e. its dark tones are overemphasized (if an image's exposure is correct, the data will be centered in the graph).

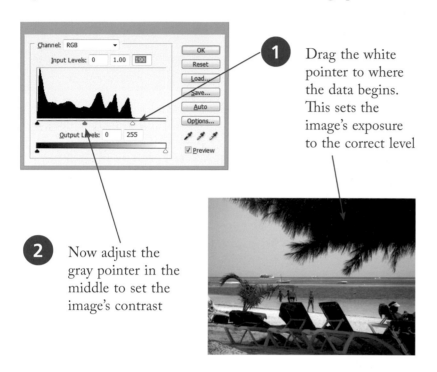

The pointer on the right controls light tones (highlights), the one on the left controls dark tones (shadows), and the middle one controls midtones (contrast).

1 Drag the white pointer to where the data begins. This sets the image's exposure to the correct level

2 Now adjust the gray pointer in the middle to set the image's contrast

If an image is over-exposed, its data will be to the right of the graph. In this case, you would drag the black slider to where the data begins.

Color Correction

The next adjustment to make is to the image's colors. This is done with the Hue/Saturation control (shown below). A common mistake is to adjust all the colors simultaneously until the picture "looks about right". However, this often results in one color being correct and the others being incorrect.

The right way to do it is to edit each color individually by selecting it from the Edit menu. Adjustments will thus affect that color only.

An example is shown on the next page.

Another, more advanced, tool that can be used for color correction is the Curves tool.

In this image, the grass and trees have a yellowish tint that gives a slightly washed-out or faded look

Adjusting green only gives the grass and trees a more natural color, while the other colors remain unchanged

Color Cast Correction

A common problem with digital photos is the image having an unwanted tint. This can also be corrected with the Hue/Saturation control. Select the color of the cast in the Edit menu and then drag the slider back to eliminate it.

Sharpening

The first rule of image sharpening is that this process is the last edit to be made. The second rule is to ignore the Sharpen and Sharpen More tools, as they provide little user control and usually result in the image being sharpened incorrectly.

The tool you should use is the Unsharp Mask. When using this, you need to zoom in closely so that you can work with precision.

Many imaging programs provide a zoom-in preview window for this purpose. If yours doesn't, use the program's zoom control to get in close.

The rule of thumb is to look for halos along sharp edges. When you see these, reduce the Threshold setting until the halos disappear. Then you should be about right.

Game Play Optimization

The average computer system is not specified highly enough to play many of today's 3D games at their optimum level. By this we mean all sound/graphic enhancements and features turned on and set at maximum. With "all guns blazing" most PCs will struggle, with gameplay being slow and jerky.

The following tips will help to prevent this:

- Reinstall the game and choose the option that installs the majority (or all) of the game's data on the hard drive. The less the game has to access the disc, the more smoothly it will run.

- Before you start the game, switch the PC off for a few seconds. Doing this will clear the memory and ensure the PC is in an optimal condition.

- When playing the game make sure no other applications are running on the PC.

- Try reducing the amount of action, e.g. reduce the number of opponents, cars in a racing game, etc. The less that is going on, the better the PC will be able to cope with the game.

- Go into the game's graphics setup options and reduce the screen resolution. Then reduce settings such as Anti-Aliasing, Shadows, and Textures. These features improve graphic quality considerably but do place a heavy load on the PC.

Typical game graphics options. Dragging the sliders back will speed up the game

- The final, and most drastic, option is to upgrade your system's hardware, i.e. the memory, and possibly the CPU and video system as well.

Before buying any 3D game, make sure your CPU and memory match its recommended system requirements. These will be somewhere on the box. You must also have the version of DirectX required by the game; otherwise it won't run properly, if at all.

Achieving a smooth level of gameplay is usually a compromise between graphics quality and performance, and will require a certain amount of trial and error.

If the game's installation options allow you to install the entire game to the hard drive, do so. Having to constantly retrieve data from the CD/DVD drive can cause the game to stutter.

Turn your PC into a TV/PVR

TV tuner hardware has advanced a long way since its early days, and it's now possible to buy these devices in the form of tiny flash drives that plug into a USB port. These often incorporate two tuners that allow you to watch one program while recording another.

What hasn't advanced is the software usually supplied with these devices. In general, these programs are OK for watching TV but nothing else.

The solution is to use third-party software such as Windows Media Center (WMC), GB-PVR and MediaPortal. WMC is a superb program that fully utilizes the capabilities of modern TV tuner hardware. Unfortunately, it not included in Windows 8.1 as it was in Vista and Windows 7. However, it is available as a paid add-on and anyone interested in using their PC as a personal video recorder (PVR) is well advised to acquire it.

Hot tip

TV tuners come in two types: analog and digital. Of the two, digital is the recommended option as it does not suffer from interference, e.g. ghosting.

WMC instantly recognizes the TV hardware the first time you run it, and then opens a setup wizard that automatically scans for available channels and configures the device. This is all done so effortlessly that it is difficult to understand why the bundled software is so slow and problematic.

Once set up, watching and recording TV with WMC is a breeze.

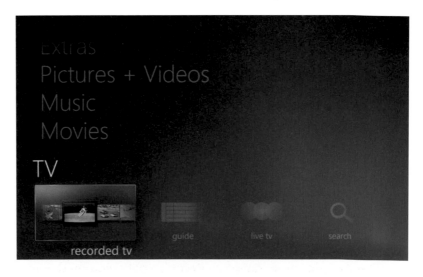

TV options in Windows Media Center

...cont'd

Click Live TV and you can watch any channel either full-screen or in a resizable window. A range of options and features, including a record button, is available at the bottom-right.

The recorded TV window shows a list of all the programs you have recorded, together with useful information such as the date of recording, channel it was recorded on, plus a brief or full outline of the plot, depending on which view you select. The latter is extremely useful when browsing programs recorded some time ago, the details of which you may have forgotten.

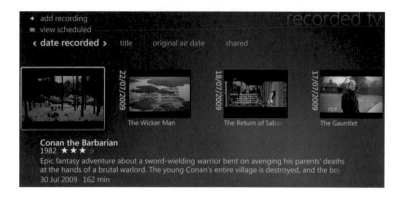

The electronic program guide (EPG) is probably the most useful feature of all. This updates automatically and allows you to look days ahead to see what programs are coming.

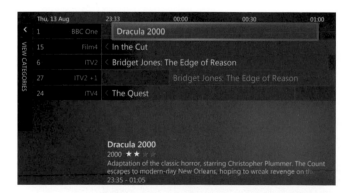

If you find one you wish to record, even if it's not due for several days, simply right-click and select Record. WMC will do the rest. Playback quality is smooth with none of the jerkiness found with other software. Image quality is excellent as well.

Multimedia Viewers

For viewing your pictures, Windows 8.1 provides Windows Photo Viewer. While this program is adequate, it does have a very limited set of features. A much better application is IrfanView.

IrfanView's already wide range of functions can be further extended by downloading free plug-ins from the manufacturer's website.

Shown above, this is a powerful imaging program that has a wide range of features – far too many to list here. Quite simply, no computer user should be without it. IrfanView is available as a free download at **www.irfanview.com**

With regard to video, Windows 8.1's offering is Windows Media Player. This is an excellent program that, unlike Photo Viewer, has a good range of features and capabilities. However, this does not include support for playing DVDs.

IrfanView and Zoom Player are both completely free of spyware and adware.

For this reason, we recommend the Zoom Player, available as a free download from **www.inmatrix. com** This media player has a clean, uncluttered interface, is very quick to load, yet has a powerful set of features. For a free application, it's unbeatable.

14 Miscellaneous

This chapter contains a number of tips that relate to both the PC and the Internet. For example, how to store your data in the cloud and sync that data across all of your devices. We also look at some handy applications that may not be apparent at first glance.

Keyboard Calculator

The calculator provided by Windows is a very handy and much-used application. However, operating it with a mouse is less than ideal as it is very easy to press the wrong button. You could never add up a column of figures at anything like the speed of a real calculator.

The tip described below allows you to do just that:

1 Press the Num Lock key on the keyboard

2 Open the calculator by typing calc in the search box

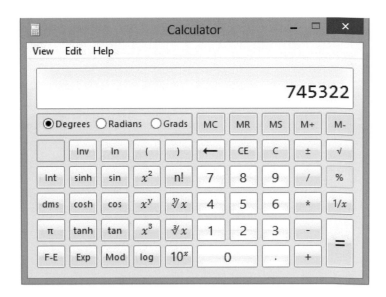

3 Instead of fiddling about with the mouse to enter numbers, simply use the numeric keypad on the right-hand side of the keyboard

Key	Action
/	The equivalent of divide
*	The equivalent of multiply
+	The equivalent of plus
-	The equivalent of minus
Enter	The equivalent of equals

Don't forget

Windows calculator can be expanded to a scientific mode. Select this option from the View menu.

Hot tip

While the calculator supplied by Windows is perfectly adequate for most needs, there are many more specialized calculators available for download from the Internet.

Restart Windows Explorer

From time to time Windows Explorer, which is the application responsible for the Taskbar and the Desktop, will crash. The result is that the Taskbar and all the Desktop icons will disappear, leaving a blank screen. With nothing to click, the user seemingly has no options with which to recover.

The solution is as follows:

1   Press Ctrl + Shift + Esc. This opens the Task Manager

To open the Task Manager when you have no access to the Taskbar, press Ctrl + Shift + Esc.

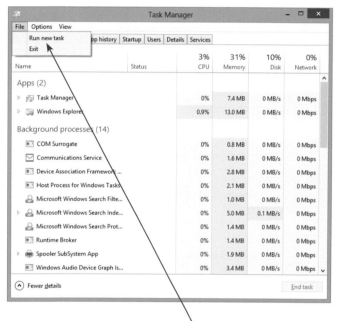

2   From the File menu, click Run new task

3   In the Open box, type explorer and then click OK

Windows will now restart Windows Explorer, which will in turn reinstate the Taskbar and the Desktop icons.

Turbo-Charge the Mouse

Many users are not aware that there are several aspects of the mouse that can be enhanced, both visually and operationally.

Pointer Speed

The first is the speed at which the pointer moves across the screen. The default setting is fine for most users but some, gamers for example, will benefit from a faster speed:

Hot tip

Clicking the Pointers tab will give you access to a range of mouse pointers. Have a look here because you may find pointers that are more suitable for your use of the PC than the default pointer.

1 Go to Control Panel and click Mouse. Then click the Pointer Options tab

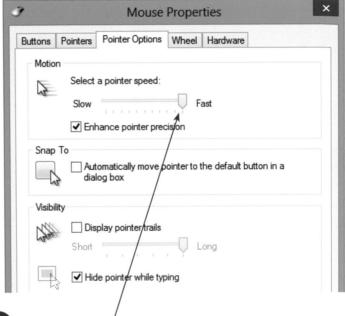

2 Drag the slider forward to increase the pointer's speed

Mouse Snap To

While you have the Pointer Options dialog box open, you can alter another setting that will change the mouse's behavior.

Enabling Snap To will eliminate the need to move your mouse to a certain extent, by making the pointer jump automatically to the default button whenever a new dialog box is opened.

Some people love this; others hate it. Give it a try.

Hot tip

Have you ever been in a situation where you have simply lost the pointer? Checking "Show location of pointer when I press the CTRL key" will enable you to find it instantly the next time.

198

Easy Reading

ClearType is a feature that was originally introduced in Windows XP, and is an anti-aliasing technique that smooths the edges of fonts, thus making them easier to read.

With XP, the feature was disabled by default; with Windows 8.1 the default setting is on. However, not many users are aware that they can tweak the level of ClearType. This can be done as described below:

1 Go to Control Panel and click Display. On the left, click "Adjust ClearType text"

2 At the first screen, click Next. At the second, select the monitor to apply the settings to (assuming you have more than one)

3 The next four screens will present you with different ClearType options

199

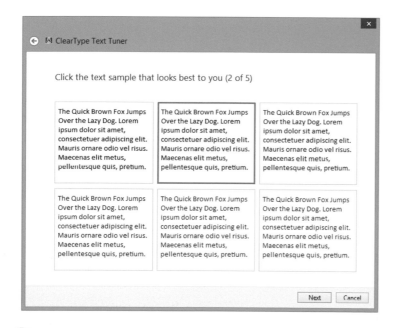

Not everybody likes ClearType. If you want to disable it, you can do so in the Display applet in the Control Panel.

If you have more than one monitor, you can apply different ClearType settings to each one.

4 Choose the setting that's best for you, click Next and then Finish

System Details

Windows provides two useful tools for users who need to get details about their system.

System Information

The first is the System Information utility. This gives detailed information about all the hardware and software on the PC. To access it, go to the Charms bar and type MSINFO32 in the Search box. Then click the Apps filter.

The main page gives a system summary that includes items such as the CPU, the amount of installed memory, details of the operating system, etc. An expandable category list on the left leads to more specific details of the system's hardware and software. System Information will also give you details about any devices that are not working properly.

Device Manager

The Device Manager, as the name suggests, allows you to view, configure, and troubleshoot the PC's hardware devices.

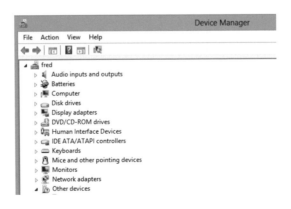

On the left is a categorized list of all the system's hardware. Expanding the categories gives details, and access to the system properties, of the individual devices.

The Device Manager also flags any devices that are not working with warning symbols, and allows you to install, and also update, device drivers.

Hot tip

The Device Manager is a very useful troubleshooting tool. If a device is flagged with a warning symbol, double-clicking it opens a dialog box that will tell you the nature of the problem, plus a suggested course of action.

Third-Party Utilities

While System Information and the Device Manager provide a lot of information about the system, there are many third-party utilities that provide greater detail. One of the best is SiSoft Sandra (shown below); this is available at **www.sisoftware.net** For really in-depth details about your system, it is a highly-recommended download.

SiSoft Sandra is available in various versions. The Lite version, which is free, will give you all the information you need.

Video and Audio Codecs

A problem that many users encounter when trying to play a video file is that they get sound but no video (or no sound in the case of a sound file). The reason is that the file's codec (see bottom margin note) is missing. To resolve the issue, they need to download and install it. The difficulty is knowing which codec is needed.

Another good utility is the Belarc Advisor. This is a free download from www.belarc.com

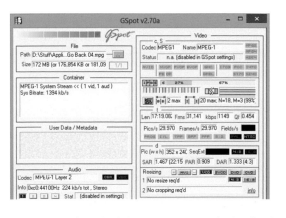

Go to **www. headbands. com/gspot** and download a program called GSpot.

Open the errant file with GSpot and you will be told not only which codec it was compressed with, but also a great deal of other information about the file. Then do a Google search for the required codec.

A codec is a program that compresses the data in sound and video files, thus reducing the size of the files. When the file is played, the same codec must be installed on the PC in order to decompress it.

Online Data Storage

In the previous edition of this book, we wrote about the plethora of websites offering online data storage facilities. Some were offering limited amounts (typically 2-5GB) for free, while larger amounts were available for a fee.

With Windows 8.1, Microsoft has jumped on this bandwagon by providing an app called OneDrive (previously called SkyDrive). This is available from the Start screen and gives users 7GB of online storage (*Correct at the time of printing.*).

To get started, click the OneDrive tile and log on with your Microsoft account. If you don't have an account, you will need to create one. Once done, you will see the following:

Hot tip

A really cool feature of OneDrive is that it is available as a "Save To" option from the file menus of many other apps and programs, such as Microsoft Office 2013.

OneDrive starts you off with a number of folders as shown above. You can create more, and also nest folders within folders. To upload and download data, click a folder to open it and then right-click to open an options bar at the bottom of the screen. This provides the relevant commands.

Features of OneDrive include: easy drag-and-drop uploading and downloading, global access to your data, and the convenience of Windows Explorer to manage your files and folders.

OneDrive does much more than just provide a place to store data, however. By integrating it with a Microsoft account, it can be used to synchronize files, photos, video, email, documents, etc., across a number of separate devices, such as PCs, smartphones, and tablets.

Problem Steps Recorder

As the local PC guru you're probably resigned to friends and family pestering you for help with their computer problems. This is bad enough, but when they are unable to clearly explain what the problem is or what they've done, as is often the case, it becomes very difficult, or even impossible, to help them.

A little known utility supplied with Windows 8.1 may provide the answer. When you get one of these irritating phone calls, tell the caller to go to their PC, type PSR in the search box and press Enter. This will open Windows 8.1's Steps Recorder.

This is useful for the reverse situation as well – trying to explain how to do something to the user. A series of screenshots indicating where to click will be much easier for an inexperienced user to follow.

Once they have this running, get them to reproduce the fault, or do whatever it was they did, again. Steps Recorder will capture every mouse click and keystroke. When they've finished, they press Stop Record and a report is generated and saved as a ZIP file. This can then be emailed to you.

When you open the report, you will see a detailed step-by-step list of every action that was made. Even more helpful is the fact that screenshots are included, as shown below:

Easy Device Management

A useful feature of Windows 8.1 is Device Stage, the purpose of which is to simplify user interaction with devices such as cell phones, printers, MP3 players, digital cameras, etc. Basically, it provides a one-stop solution for managing all tasks related to the device in question. It works as follows:

Go to Control Panel, Devices and Printers. You will see a set of high-resolution icons for all the devices connected to your PC, as shown below:

Click a device icon and a new window will open, from where you can access settings for the device and its features. In the example below, we see the author's Sony Walkman MP3 player. At the top we can see how much charge is in the battery and how much storage space is available on the device. At the bottom are various settings that enable the device's contents to be managed. The options available vary according to the type of device.

You can also access your devices from the Taskbar. When you connect one to the PC, an icon will appear on the Taskbar. Left-clicking it opens the window above. If you right-click it, you will see a jump list (see left) of the options available in the main window.

Hot tip

Not all devices work with Device Stage. Support for the feature must be built in to the device by the manufacturer.

Tasks

- Import pictures and videos
- Manage media on your de...
- Browse files
- Change general settings

- Close all windows

Reset your Computer

We saw on page 125 that the traditional method of completely restoring a Windows PC to its factory settings is to do a clean installation. This wipes the drive clean of all data, after which a new copy of Windows is installed. This is done by booting the PC from the installation disk – a procedure that most users will be wary of trying.

Windows 8.1 provides a much simpler method of restoring Windows to its factory settings. This is courtesy of its Reset utility. It works as described below:

1 From the Charms bar go to Settings, Change PC settings, Update & recovery, Recovery. Under "Remove everything and reinstall Windows", click Get started

2 At the first screen, click Next. At the second, you will be presented with two options as shown below

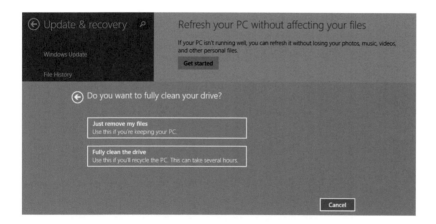

Choose the first, "Just remove my files" if you just want to start again from scratch. All the data you have put on the PC will be deleted, leaving you with a "as new" copy of Windows.

The second option, "Fully clean the drive", does the same as the first but also wipes the drive securely so the user's data cannot be subsequently recovered. This is something that is usually done when a PC is being sold or scrapped.

3 Select the required option and then sit back as Windows is restored

PC Recovery Options

Windows 8.1 is a very stable and reliable operating system. However, it will inevitably go wrong on occasion and so users need to be aware of steps they can take to resolve any issues they experience.

If the problem is not too serious and the user can still get into Windows, the procedure is as follows:

 Go to the Charms bar, Settings, Change PC settings, Update & recovery, Recovery. Under Advanced startup, click Restart now. The following screen will open:

2 Clicking Troubleshoot will present you with three options – Refresh your PC, Reset your PC, and Advanced options. The first two we have already covered on pages 38-40 and 205 respectively. Clicking Advanced options will give you a list of other troubleshooting steps as shown below:

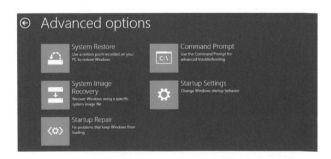

System Restore enables the PC to be restored to the state it was in when the restore point was made. This is ideal for resolving minor issues – see page 208.

System Image Recovery is similar to System Restore in that it restores the PC from an image file to a previous state. However, it is a more drastic step as it destroys all the user's data, unlike System Restore. Accordingly, it is a "last resort" option to be used only when all others have failed.

Startup Repair attempts to resolve issues that are preventing the PC from starting. So if your PC won't boot up, this is the option to try first.

Command Prompt is for advanced users and most people should leave this alone.

Startup Settings provides a list of further troubleshooting options, such as Safe Mode, Low-Resolution Video Mode, Boot Logging and more.

If the problem is so serious that you cannot get Windows running at all, you will have to access the recovery options a different way.

If you have a Windows 8.1 installation disk, the recovery options will be available from this. Configure the PC to boot from the CD/DVD drive as described on page 125, place the installation disk in the drive and then boot the PC. When the installation screen opens, you will see a "Repair this PC" option at the bottom. Click this and the recovery options will open.

However, there is a good chance you won't have an installation disk as many PCs these days are sold without one – if this is the case you will have to create a recovery disk. Windows provides you with an option to do this. However, you need to do it while your PC is functional – it's no good waiting until it has failed.

Do it by going to the Control Panel and clicking Recovery. Select the first option "Create a recovery drive" and simply follow the prompts. Note that you will need a USB drive for this.

Hot tip

If you don't have a Windows 8.1 installation disk, be sure to create a recovery drive – you might need it one day!

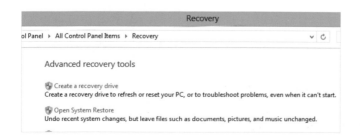

System Restore points can occupy several gigabytes of disk space. If you find yourself running low, consider deleting some of them as explained on page 31.

Configuration options for System Restore can be found by going to Control Panel, System, System Protection.

System Restore

When a computer is new, it is fast and responsive and everything works as it should. Fast-forward a few months and it will already have begun to slow down and develop minor but probably irritating problems.

Very few users have the technical knowledge to be able to resolve Windows faults, so Windows includes a utility known as System Restore. This can be used to create a restore point that is basically a snapshot, or image, of the PC at a given point.

Should the PC subsequently develop a fault that the user cannot fix, the PC can be restored from the restore point:

1 Open System Restore as described on page 206

2 Choose a restore point made at a time prior to the fault manifesting itself. Click Next and the utility will restore your system from the restore point selected

Install Java

Java is a modern technology that is used in a multitude of applications, e.g. utilities, games, and business applications. It is found on millions of computers around the world, and on billions of devices, such as smartphones, tablets, games consoles and TVs.

Java is also used extensively on websites and, without it, many of the web applications that users take for granted just won't work. Typical examples are online games, calendars, calculators, etc. It's also integral to the intranet applications and e-business solutions that are the basis of computing in the corporate world.

Internet Explorer 11, however, comes without Java. So users who access the Internet frequently need to install it themselves. Fortunately, Java is free and can be downloaded from the manufacturer, Sun Microsystems, at **www.java.com**

Java provides a platform for the development of applications that work on multiple operating systems. Essentially, that means a program written in Java will run on any type of computing platform.

Some Java applications, such as animated 3D online games, require a lot of system resources and so users with under-powered computers may find it beneficial to turn Java off when browsing certain sites.

This can be done by clicking the Tools icon at the top-right of Internet Explorer and then clicking Manage add-ons. Find the Java entry, right-click and select Disable.

If your browser is not Java-enabled, when you visit a site that uses Java you will just see a blank space where the Java applet is positioned.

Be on Time with Windows

The timekeeping utility provided with Windows 8.1 has two cool features that many users will find useful.

Additional Clocks
The first one enables you to have up to three clocks all set to different time zones:

1 Click the clock in the notification area and then click "Change date and time settings"

2 Click the Additional Clocks tab

3 Using the drop-down boxes, select the time zones you want for each clock. Then enter a display name

4 Hover the pointer over the system clock to see all the clocks

5 Click the system clock to see a larger view, plus the calendar

Reset the Clock Accurately
The usual method of resetting the PC's clock involves clicking little arrows, which is fiddly. There's also no guarantee that your reference clock is accurate. Windows provides an easier way that is also extremely accurate.

Repeat Step 1 above and then click the Internet Time tab. Click Change settings and from the drop-down box, select a time server.

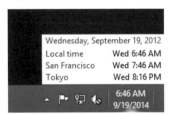

Then click the Update now button.

All of the time servers used by Windows Time utility are synchronized with atomic clocks to guarantee accuracy.

Index

I

J

K

L

M

216